The Improv Illusionist

T0269684

The Improv Illusionist

Using Object Work, Environment, and Physicality in Performance

David Raitt

methuen | drama
LONDON • NEW YORK • OXFORD • NEW DELHI • SYDNEY

METHUEN DRAMA
Bloomsbury Publishing Plc
50 Bedford Square, London, WC1B 3DP, UK
1385 Broadway, New York, NY 10018, USA
29 Earlsfort Terrace, Dublin 2, Ireland

BLOOMSBURY, METHUEN DRAMA and the Methuen Drama logo are
trademarks of Bloomsbury Publishing Plc

First published in Great Britain 2023

Cover design: Ben Anslow
Cover images: Boy in Pirate Costume with Shovel (© invincible_bulldog / iStock);
Fighting samurai icon. (© Nsit / Shutterstock); Female baseball players isolated
characters vector set (© Wanlee / Adobe Stock)

A catalogue record for this book is available from the British Library.

A catalog record for this book is available from the Library of Congress.

ISBN HB: 978-1-3503-2638-5
PB: 978-1-3503-2637-8
ePDF: 978-1-3503-2640-8
eBook: 978-1-3503-2639-2

Typeset by Deanta Global Publishing Services, Chennai, India
Printed and bound in Great Britain

To find out more about our authors and books visit www.bloomsbury.com and
sign up for our newsletters.

For

Amy and Duncan
Who helped me find my voice

And

My wonderful family
Who have always encouraged me using it.

Contents

Foreword

by Bruce Hunter

When I first witnessed good improvisation, it floored me. It was so raw and exciting. That energy in the room when everyone is experiencing the immediacy of the moment, collectively and firsthand, is breathtaking. It was like an iconic rock show that lives in your mind forever. And I don't think that experience was unique to just me. I know many others who have felt this joy when improv is done well. What I was feeling was freedom. Freedom from the social structures that ruled most of our lives. Free from the rules of written material. Free of any constructs that would appear to hold you back. A feeling of *anything goes* and that anything can happen. What I was watching was jazz.

We all know jazz doesn't come easy. It takes years of practice to learn everything you can about the rules and how to break them. It is a delight to see performers break new ground with such grace and skill and create new worlds, much like improvisers do. What couldn't be done moments before now becomes possible.

Now let me be clear about social structures so I don't get labeled an anarchist. Under the rules of living, certain social norms are expected like how to "not rock the boat." As we all know, it is in the "rocking of the boat" that the humor normally lies within. I would call it *the spanner in the works*. This is where we need to break free of societal structures—of being "nice"— to find the interesting bits.

Like all good story structures, *The Who* (Who is this character? What pond or swamp did they just flop in from? How do they feel about the world around them? Are they low status or high status? Are they a threat to the status quo? What do they want? Etc.) and *The What* (What is the scene about? What is being threatened? What is being lost or gained? Etc.) affect and create a scene.

But so often overlooked is *The Where*. I have always felt that *The Where* is the most important element. Not enough attention is paid to the skill of creating environment. Certainly, it is one of the best for creating comedy onstage. Environment dictates action and thusly its limitations. Where you are usually informs what you are doing. When we see an improviser start to type our brain creates the environment around them. It becomes clear that they are in an office or on a spacecraft—when the character sees it, we see it. Environments, to a skilled improviser, can become their greatest tool. Watching a football team practice in the locker room because it's raining outside is great fodder for material, especially if you're good at creating environments. Watching a room full of football players try to collectively watch the same mimed football is funny. Especially if they fail watching the same ball and one of them asks, "How many balls are we playing with?"

In my classes, I would ask someone to create an environment and inevitably they would open the fridge door and grab a beer. Then they'd stand there with the beer, not sure what to do next. In most cases they would forget they were even holding the beer. So, we learn that simply creating the environment is not enough—you have to be affected by the environment you create. If we really lean into environment, it can feed us all kinds of great ideas. For example, does that beer get empty quickly and this poor sap has no place to put it down? Watching this character trying to be polite with the empty bottle becomes fodder. Does he try to hide it? Do people keep noticing him when he's about to hide it? Does he get caught and start playing it like a flute? Just a simple choice from the environment can create mountains of material. Being aware environmentally always saved me on stage.

Mime technique is also a great asset in creating new worlds. Mime is not a skill that comes easy, but even half-assed attempts can be rewarding on an improv stage. Done well, it can take a scene to a whole new level. Look at Buster Keaton and Charlie Chaplin: their attention to physicality and timing was impeccable. They understood the limitations of the physical world and we laughed as they mocked it and themselves living in it.

I found mime to be very inspiring for my work. (If it was good enough for David Bowie, it was good enough for me.) It served me very well when I improvised and then went on to teach improvisation and acting; it helped me to understand the world around me and my connection to the environment. It also prepared me for future work as a puppeteer. (Shout-out to Ron East and the Mime School Unlimited.)

Whether working with the immediate environment (the world around you, what you can touch, the pen you hold, the coffee you drink, the empty beer bottle), the general environment (shared space between the characters), or the larger environment (places outside of the room), possibilities come out of your attention to environment and the detail within those choices:

1. The improv scene is funnier when the assistant's pen keeps running out of ink. And he has to bang it on the table to get it to work every time his boss tries to give him some instruction.
2. Is the neighbor's wife hiding in the bathroom while you converse with her husband?

Improvisers live for these moments of discovery, and audiences love it.

As I said, *The Where* is my favorite. I even started a theatre company whose shows are based entirely on real environments. *The What* can change in seconds, *The Who* might change or realize something if they don't die first, but *The Where* takes the reality of it all and grinds your face into it until you can only mock it. But know this: it is your lover. Embrace it and it will serve you well, deny it and it will kill you in your sleep long before your head even hits the pillow.

I love that David Raitt has taken on this focus because he understands the importance of environment, detail, and the skills you need to be your best. He has brought his great experience, worthy insight, and unique practices to help make improvisers do wonderfully funny things for future audiences. Well done, Dave. I wish you and all your readers great laughs.

With great respect,
Bruce Hunter

Bruce Hunter is an improviser, actor, teacher, mime artist, puppeteer, writer, director, and theatre maker. He is a Co-Founder & Artistic Director of RealSpace Theatre, online at https://realspacetheatre.wordpress.com/

Acknowledgments

Improv is teamwork. This may be my book, but you're only reading it because the following people helped turn me into who I am.

Amy and Duncan McKenzie, and Gary Pearson founded Oakville Improv, which couldn't be a better home company for me. I'm forever indebted to them for their advice and friendship. Without it, I might never have realized my potential as a physical improviser.

Many years before that, Bruce Hunter was my first, best teacher of environment, object work, and physicality, laying the foundation for my entire improv career. It's a huge honor to have him contribute the Foreword to this book.

I've also learned so much from other teachers and directors: Shari Hollett, Chris Earle, Michael Kennard, Paul O'Sullivan, Nick Johne, Bruce Pirrie, Sandra Balcovske, Lisa Merchant, Jerry Schaefer, and Joe Flaherty. (Yes, *that* Joe Flaherty.)

Lyn Okkerse took a chance on hiring me for The Second City Toronto. Later on, Steve Morel and Klaus Schuller did the same thing. I'm grateful for every moment of my time there, and for my friendships with its actors, crew, and bar staff.

For seventeen years, The Second City Education Company helped me grow as a teacher. Thanks to Jody Bishop, Kevin Frank, Paul Shoebridge, and Lanrick Bennett, Jr., for every opportunity to practice.

My Improv Illusions students have helped me make the ideas in this book stronger with their feedback, questions, and hard work.

I've improvised with hundreds of professional and amateur performers, and learned something from everyone, even if it's only that improv is a blast. I hate that I can't list all their names here, but I'd hate more to leave anyone out by mistake. Here's hoping I get the chance to thank you all individually.

I do have to mention Geri Hall, who not only read and commented on an early draft but is one of the nicest people you'll ever meet.

Thanks again to Kaci Beeler for her important contributions to the Emotional Safety chapter. I hope I've done justice to the important work she and many others are contributing to our theatres.

Thank you to everyone at Bloomsbury for their support of this project, especially Anna Brewer, Aanchal Vij, and Sam Nicholls. Christine Pillman helped my grammar, enjoys talking about commas, and is a fun improv partner. I wouldn't have finished this book without Tim Clare and Jane Friedman, and I highly recommend their online resources.

As always, thanks to my family, especially Tracy, Billy, and JC. Your love and encouragement are my fuel.

Introduction

Have you ever seen a good magic act? How did it make you feel?

When a magician does a great trick, it drives the audience wild. They gasp; they laugh; they scream. And they demand to know "*How did you do that?*"

Have you ever had that experience performing for an *improv* audience?

You can. Because improv is magic, and all improvisers are magicians. You create stories, characters, and worlds from nothing. And when you really connect—like ingeniously calling back an idea, or saying a perfectly timed line—it drives the audience wild. They gasp; they laugh; they scream. And they demand to know "*How did you do that?*"

The most potent form of magic is *illusion*—the power to make people see what isn't there. All improvisers are illusionists. Using your skills, you create objects, activities, and environments on an empty stage. You can fix a broken photocopier in one moment, wrangle cattle across the open range in the next, and then explore a planet near Betelgeuse. Audiences are spellbound by these illusions. They accept them as absolutely real.

But watch out! If you're careless, your illusions break the reality of your improvisation. You walk through tables and closed doors. You put objects down in one place and pick them up somewhere else. You think your scene is about doing the laundry, but your partner sees you feeding a goat. The audience becomes confused, detached, maybe even resentful.

This book is about the major tools of the Improv Illusionist: *object work, environment, and physicality*. These tools do more than just control what people see. They help you add depth and dimension to your characters and narrative. They also open up new sources of ideas, which bring even more magic to your performances.

Ready to explore the improv illusion? Splendid! Step right through here.

Where This Book Came From

All my life I've loved physically expressive theatre, film, and sketch comedy. In my first improv classes, I was especially drawn to object work and environment. I learned their importance not only to a scene but also to giving the audience more to look at—a real *show*. As a result, my improv approach has always been very physical. Over the years, however, I've had trouble finding instruction in anything more than the basic concepts.

There are many learning options in the physical theatre, including dance, mime, clown, and bouffon. All of these use improvisation (at least in rehearsal) to explore storytelling through movement. But they're not to everyone's taste, and I never found they connected with the type of unscripted theatre I wanted to perform. So I had to figure it out for myself. I researched exercises for adding more detail and visual flair to performance. I broke down the physics of movement, trying to understand how the improv illusion works. I tracked down other physical players and shared ideas.

And I tried to find great books. If you love improvisation like I do, you probably have a shelf full of books, including *Impro*, *Truth in Comedy*, *The Improv Handbook*, and a dozen others.[1] The problem is, while most great improv books mention exploring the environment for ideas, they're very short on practical techniques. They discuss the importance of the "Where" in establishing a platform, but refer to object work only in passing. Even books that claim to be "the ultimate guide to improvisation" may have only a very short chapter about these topics. There's a huge information gap here.

Several years ago, some friends and I got to talking about physicality in improv. There is so much wasted potential! North American improv has become stereotyped as all about clever dialogue and fast and funny jokes. In any given show, I see a lot of scenes where characters stand and talk, with

---

[1] There are more I'd recommend, but this is only the Introduction and already we're down a rabbit hole. Check out the Improv Illusionist website for my list. https://improvillusionist.com/books/

little sense of place or visual interest. Many friends told me that they *wanted* to be "more physical" but weren't sure how to do it. They'd noticed the information gap, too.

Soon after, I began teaching my approach, drawing from all my influences and experimenting with different exercises. The goal of my *Improv Illusionist* workshops is to bring object work, environment, and physicality back into every improviser's toolbox.

They say authors write the books they wish they had when starting out. For me, this is that book. I hope it's not the last. I'd love to see more exploration of physical improv in the future.

The Basics and Beyond

"A whole book about object work and environment? Isn't that just beginner stuff? Surely there's not that much to it."

You'd be forgiven for thinking this way if your improv education followed the common pattern. Establishing the Where is one of the first skills improvisers learn, because it helps them create strong platforms to tell stories. Unfortunately, many training programs treat environment work as "the basics" and then leave it behind. As students move on to "advanced" concepts such as character and narrative, they're never shown how environment fits in as an equal partner. And, since some of these students become teachers, and some of those go on to write improv books of their own, this explains why the information is so thin.

Worse, improvisers get out of practice with object work, and it begins to feel awkward and uncomfortable. Some players respond by avoiding it altogether, which creates another problem—their scenes are all talking heads. This not only gives the audience little to look at, it's also much harder on the players. When you avoid physicality, you have to think harder to make your scenes feel different from each other.

To be fair, you can still perform good improv *without* environment. Physical play doesn't solve everything, and it's not something you can (or should) always turn to. When you forget the foundations, however, you develop bad habits. And this is especially true with object work.

So yes, this book does cover the basics. But what I've learned about environment can take your improv further. I'll also show you how to use it to generate ideas, develop richer stories, and solve problems that come up in your improvisations. With a well-rounded skill set, you'll be able to give your audience a more spectacular performance.

You'll also learn about Physical and Emotional Safety for performers, which is another information gap in improv training. And I've included some practical tips for the working improviser, useful for players at any experience level.

Along the way, I'll illustrate with stories and insights from my long career as a student, professional performer, director, and instructor.

One important point: while there's lots here that beginners can learn about physical improv, this is *not* a book for learning to improvise generally. If you're very new to improv, I suggest you read the books I mentioned above, or even better, try a few introductory classes. Once you understand the basics of improvised storytelling, come back here to learn how to bring more physicality into your performance.

Influences and Styles

Improv is like philosophy—there are many different schools of thought and much debate over the "right" one. Many students ask me what style I teach. What I call "physical improv" isn't a style, it's a set of tools you can use any way you like. It's a *multiplier* that gives you more options and more ideas. It makes you more expressive, more involving, more entertaining.

But it may help you to know my influences, since they inform the language and explanations I use in this book. My first improv teachers were veterans of Theatresports and Calgary's Loose Moose Theatre Company,[2] so my basic training followed the Keith Johnstone model. I'm a graduate of the introductory and Conservatory programs at The Second City Toronto, and performed for their Canadian National Touring Company and Mainstage (ensemble) for four years. I was also a member of The Second City Education faculty for seventeen years.

If you don't know (or care) what any of that means, great! Physical improv is useful for performers at any level who want to create richer environments in their improvisation. You can use these tools for any improv format you

---

[2] This includes the amazing Bruce Hunter, who generously contributed the Foreword to this book. Bruce was my first improv mentor, and I highly recommend you study from him if you ever get a chance.

prefer: short-form, long-form, performance games, genre improv, "bar-prov," and so on.

Even if you subscribe to a particular "style"—Second City, Annoyance, UCB, Match, or any type of "modern" improv[3]—environment work is universal. Regardless of how we tell stories, so much of who we are and how we relate to others is tied to places and activities. It makes sense to build the skills to convey these to an audience.

If you enjoy and use a lot of movement in performance, people may call you a "physical improviser." That's not really a definition of style, and environment work is about more than physical movement. While it's true that we create improvised props mostly through moving the hands and body, there are other techniques available. You'll see that even players with mobility challenges can draw their audience into powerful illusions.

In fact, environment work is so universal, it can even be used in scripted theatre. Minimalist productions can use object work when budget or artistic choices limit the use of props.

Meet the Mother of Improv

My greatest influence in this work is Viola Spolin. She's known (at least in North America) as "the Mother of Improv" for her contributions to improvisation. Beginning in the 1920s, she used games as tools for stimulating creative expression in children and adults. Later, she expanded this work into teaching both formal and improvisational theatre. Along with her son, Paul Sills, she taught most of the original actors at The Second City Chicago. And we all know what that led to.[4]

Even if you've never heard of Viola, you've likely played many of the theatre games she created. Her major book, *Improvisation for the Theater*, lists over 200 exercises. Many are classics taught around the world, including *Mirror*, *Space Walk*, and *Transformation of Objects*. Some have been co-opted for short-form performance, such as *Dubbing* and *Gibberish Interpreter*. If you haven't read Viola's work, I highly recommend you add it to your library.

---

[3] My apologies to international improvisers if this list seems exclusively North American. However, I do find there's more debate over improv styles in the United States and Canada than in other countries.
[4] If you want to learn more about Spolin's fascinating life and work, look online for *Inventing Improv*, a 2021 documentary from PBS.

Some improvisers criticize Spolin's games as limited in use, because they don't teach scene work or long-form narrative. That misses the point. The games aren't actually meant to teach you to improvise. They use improv to solve specific problems of theatrical focus, such as emotion, character, or acting with the whole body. These are the tools of the actor. And since improvisation *is* acting, regardless of style or format, everyone should regularly practice with Spolin games to keep those tools sharp. (Yes, even you bar-prov jokesters.) How you apply your actor's tools in improv performance is up to you.

Viola used games to stimulate what she called "direct experience." The goal is to get out of our heads, away from thinking, and experience an improvisation in the moment. This, she said, is where we become the most intuitive and spontaneous. It's not surprising that many of her games involve the Where. Turning your focus to objects and activities is an easy and natural way of getting out of your head. This also explains why the environment can be a constant source of inspiration.

I regularly use Spolin games in my workshops and have included some of her ideas and exercises in this book. But you should know that I'm not a Spolin purist. My issue with her teaching method is her approach to evaluation. After an exercise, she preferred only to report her observations and inquire if the players successfully held the intended focus. She left it up to the students to work out how to do it through their own experience. She felt that actors solving problems on their own was more effective for skill-building than a lecture from the teacher.

For the most part, I agree that's a sound approach. Because everyone's body is different, improvisers do need to find their own path into their physicality. However, if we expect students to make all their own physical discoveries, they might miss some easy and practical techniques for communicating environment to an audience. To give players more tools to work with, I teach these techniques alongside Spolin's games. I don't adapt her work, but I do try to supplement it.

How to Learn Improv from a Book

You can't, really. To understand improv, you need to do it—in shows, workshops, or even by yourself. Practicing the skills trains your mind for improvisational communication.

Of course, books are fantastic for learning new ideas, techniques, and exercises. With a book, I can share all kinds of information I think will help your performance. The problem is, I can't dialogue with you or change the words I've used to explain things. It's up to YOU to figure out how my ideas fit with *your* improv.

To make the most of this (or any) book, don't be a passive reader. Try the exercises. Challenge the ideas. Make notes on the pages. Discuss concepts with your fellow players. Connect them to your previous improv experiences, and make plans to try new things.

I want to help you turn ideas into instincts. Throughout the book, I attempt to describe how you might free-associate ideas as you navigate an improvisation. Over my career, I've found these *thought experiments* are great for training your mind for performance. Cognitive science research shows that mental rehearsal can often be just as effective as an actual experience. Obviously, you and I think differently, so you need to reflect on how you would explore the same process in a scene.

Think about your mindset right now, as you start the book. What are you here for? What do you want to learn? What do you *think* you'll learn? Ask these questions often—they'll draw your attention to the information that will be most useful to you.

About the Exercises

Throughout the book, I've included some favorite exercises and games for teaching object work, environment, and physicality. They're in shaded boxes like this one so you can spot them easily when flipping through. And there's a full list with page references in the Appendix. Many of the exercises are classics, and some are experimental ones I've made up. You might know them by different names—similar games often have local variations.

Part I

Foundations

---

1 Why Bother with Environment?
2 First Principles

I'm sure you want to dive into the practical chapters, especially if you're an experienced improviser. But you'll get a lot more out of the rest of this book if you absorb a bit of theory and background first.

You Will Learn

- why object work, environment, and physicality are so important to improvisation; and
- important First Principles that will define this work and help you avoid problems.

1

Why Bother with Environment?

Physical improv is powerful. Think back on your most memorable improv moments, scenes you've seen or played yourself. I'm willing to bet you'll recall more that involved physical action than clever lines of dialogue. But even dialogue-only moments often get their power from the context provided by physicality.

And yet, environment still languishes as "beginner stuff." Improvisers talk about object work like it's boring, a necessary chore to get through a scene. Others deliberately avoid environment, perhaps because they feel they need Marcel Marceau-level mime skills to do it. (You don't.)

You may still be wondering why this is such a big deal. Who cares if your object work is sloppy? Why go further than the basics of setting up a location?

If I'm going to suggest you commit to more physical play, it makes sense to point out the benefits. So here's why environment matters, along with a few previews of what you'll learn later in this book.

Elevate the Art

When you play shows in a church basement or a loud pub, it's easy to forget that improv is *theatre*. And great theatre is magical. Have you ever seen a play where the curtain opens to reveal an elaborate world? Sometimes the audience gasps and applauds before the action even begins. With more physicality in your presentation, you *can* achieve this same type of reaction in improvisation.

Does that sound too grandiose? Well, consider improv's reputation as "disposable theatre." If we want people to remember, return to, and tell their friends about our shows, we need to convince them it's more than silly make-em-ups. Comic or serious, if we want to elevate improv to a respected art form, we need to bring more actor's tools into our performance. Physicality is one of the biggest.

Stun the Crowd

It's easier to make audiences laugh when they're caught up in the world of your story. A sense of place draws them in. They care more about your character's problem when they see it in the context of your surroundings.

Over the years I've seen plenty of examples, but one especially comes to mind. One night at Toronto's Bad Dog Theatre Company, I was in the audience for a tournament match featuring ILLUSIONOID,[1] the team of Paul Bates, Lee Smart, and Nug Nahrgang. I worked with them for many years through The Second City Toronto—they're true professionals.

ILLUSIONOID is all about long-form, retro science fiction.[2] That night, their story was about a team of scientists tracking down a mysterious artifact

---

[1] Great name—just a coincidence with the title of my book!
[2] They also have a very funny improvised podcast. https://www.illusionoid.com/

to defend the world from an alien invasion. On getting a lead to its possible location, Lee said, *"To the Bubble Car!"*

Instantly, the three cut to a bizarre vehicle speeding across the landscape. It was a massive thing, the kind of hybrid speeder-tank you see in classic Japanese anime. It had levels, a cockpit, an observation dome, and a pedal-powered propulsion system. It was really only a single chair and the movement of three skilled improvisers, but we could all *see it in detail*.

Well, the crowd went nuts. An explosion of laughter and applause hit the theatre, and it went on for many seconds. People were still talking about it on the way out of the show. I'm still talking about it now.

Improv audiences are *the best*. They're patient, forgiving, and usually willing to go where we take them, even if it leads nowhere. Most importantly, they accept the blank stage. We can stand rooted to the spot, trading witty banter, and audiences will watch. They might even be entertained.

However, there's a reason we call it a *Show*. People go to theatre and movies to see things outside of their normal experience. And life doesn't unfold in a placeless void. By giving our scenes locations, objects, and activities, we pull the audience further into the experience.

Until moments like the Bubble Car happen, we forget how powerful environment and object work are. It's not only grand set pieces that hold this power. Clear, specific details help our scenes come to life in subtle ways too. Everything becomes more *real*.

Support your partners, build on ideas, and the audience will enjoy the show. Give them something to *see* and they will *love* you for it. Even though there's nothing actually there.

An added bonus is *longevity*. People tend to remember what they see more than the words they hear. If you want audiences to remember your scenes (and you), add more visual elements. I can't actually remember what the Bubble Car story was about, what the characters said, or how it ended. But I can still recall that visual moment and the audience reaction.

Find More Play

Watch kids on a playground and you'll see some amazing natural improvisation. They don't care about narrative, conflict, or Game of the scene. They live in their imaginary worlds. To them, that play structure *is* an ice castle, that tree *is* a spaceship, and the ground *is* lava. And in those worlds, they play out some wonderful stories.

The improv we practice on stage is no different from those "let's pretend" games we used to play. But we grown-ups get caught in our heads. We think too much about original characters, complex stories, nuanced ideas. And we want the audience to love us. Add in a sedentary lifestyle and a touch of self-doubt, and physicality becomes even more difficult. The result is a whole lot of wooden, talking-head scenes.

Improv philosophy encourages us to *just play*. What better way to do that than by going back to the way kids do it?

Commit to exploring environment in your scenes, and the stage becomes your playground. That's not a box or bentwood chair you're sitting on—it's a bed. And what can you do with a bed? Sleep? Jump on it? Pillow fight? Can you use those actions to express the emotions of your character? Can they affect the narrative?

Sometimes you want to be plain goofy. I love putting stairs or ladders into my scenes and then running up and down them, for no reason other than to inject a little fun.

A sense of play helps you add energy and do unpredictable things. It stretches your body and your versatility. Environment helps you reclaim it.

Try this exercise sometime:

Follow the Leader/Boot Camp/Tough Mudder

Imagine the space as a playground or army base or obstacle race. Players follow a leader up, down, over, and under various obstacles. Play with how you pass by these obstacles, but try to keep things consistent—the same size, shape, and in the same place. The leader should be mindful of mobility and flexibility issues in the class. This one is VERY physical.

Be an Awesome Scene Partner

You can get ideas from the environment even if you're not the one doing the object work. One simple move from a great partner can open up a whole world of ideas for you.

I did a scene once where my partner (can't remember who, unfortunately) and I were a couple chatting over a glass of wine. I hadn't really thought about where we were. If you'd stopped us and asked, I might have said we were at her apartment, or a generic restaurant. Then, to refill our glasses, she reached down and took the bottle out of a cooler at her feet. I immediately got the sense that we were outside in the park, which then gave me an emotional response—I was worried we'd get caught by the cops for drinking in public. She countered by complaining I wasn't adventurous enough. It developed into a fantastic relationship scene where we dared each other to do more and more outrageous things in a public place. (And the cops did end up catching us in the end.) All traced back to a quick little object move.

Improv is about making your scene partner look good. When you explore the environment, you're giving them a sense of place that helps inform their choices. The ideal improv partner has a well-rounded skill set that includes physicality.

Get Out of Your Head

Improvisation feels easier and more natural when you stay present. You're more observant of your partner's offers and more flexible to respond. Thinking or planning too much is dangerous because it turns your focus inward, distracting you from what's going on. You miss opportunities to react intuitively and honestly.

We call this *being stuck in your head*. It can happen to any of us, at any time, for any number of reasons: fear, fatigue, an unexpected offer, distractions from the audience. It can be a downward spiral. You feel detached from the scene, so you work harder to focus, which feels hard, which makes you think harder, and so on. In extreme cases, being stuck in your head can lead to panic. You might steamroll the scene, making wild offers to wrestle back control. Or you might freeze up, with no idea what to do next.

In her excellent book, *The Improviser's Way*, Katy Schutte points out that being in your head isn't necessarily a bad thing. The audience can't see when it's happening, and they will enjoy a show just as much. Some nights, you just have to work harder. But it's helpful to have a way to get out of your head and back into the flow of a scene.

One of Viola Spolin's favorite side-coaching phrases was *"Out of the head, into the space."* She knew that focusing on space objects directly (instead of thinking about creating them) was the best way to access your intuition. Anytime you find yourself in your head, exploring the environment can help you focus outward again.

In Part IV, I'll present some techniques for problem-solving—how to quickly generate ideas to get a scene back on track. But if you practice environment work enough that it becomes instinctive, you may find you get stuck in your head less often.

Use More of Your Brain

Before improv became my life's work, I studied Cognitive Science at university. I love learning about how the brain works and how we might use this knowledge to make our lives easier—including in improvisation.

One interesting research area is the study of brain activation through movement. You experience thoughts as a result of patterns of electrical stimulation in various parts of your brain. When you move around, more brain areas are activated, which increases the potential for meaningful electrical patterns to arise. This explains the common experience of getting new ideas while taking a walk, or in the shower.[3]

So, adding more physicality to performance—as opposed to those static, talky scenes—could help stimulate your creativity. It's just a theory, but to get more of your brain working when you're on stage and constantly searching for ideas? Yes, please!

Speaking of how the brain works, in Chapter 3 we'll talk about the science of mime and how we put different perceptions together to identify objects. This will help you understand how to add more detail to object work, so your partners and audience can clearly read what you're doing. (And prevent them from mis-reading, too.)

The Audience Sees Everything

When a player breaks reality in a scene, say by walking through the space where a table was established, you can often *feel* a reaction go through the audience. But why should this be? Why does the casual audience member

---

[3] This is a simplification, of course. Describing this research in detail would take us way off topic. If you're curious about the science and its applications, a fascinating book is *The Extended Mind* by Annie Murphy Paul.

always seem to notice things that the experienced improvisers on stage miss?

At the start of a scene, everyone (improvisers and audience) has one goal: to figure out what's happening. Anything said or done could be important later, so we all pay close attention to every detail, no matter how small. However, while the improvisers are working to turn this information into something, the audience is simply watching. They've got a lot more freedom to note what they've seen. From their seats in the house, they also have a wider perspective of everything happening on the stage.

If your object work is even slightly offset from what the audience has previously seen, their minds flag the difference. Most of the time it's no big deal—they make a quick mental adjustment and carry on. The more it keeps happening, though, the more it calls their attention to the improvisers instead of the scene. This is when we lose them. They may not criticize, but they're definitely not involved.

Especially with environment, we're always at a disadvantage to the audience. Practicing our skills helps us remember details and place them consistently. If we pay careful enough attention, we benefit by keeping the crowd immersed in our scenes.

Look Like a Genius

In many ways, the audience does a lot of narrative work for us. Like all humans, their minds are wired to create stories by connecting separate actions together. When you improvise, each new action you take creates an open loop. When you close a loop by reincorporating past actions, it's extremely satisfying. You're integrating everything into the story.

Establishing objects in a scene gives you all sorts of opportunities for reincorporation. For example, if I enter an office with a heavy box, and then later the building catches on fire, I can pick up the box and use it to break a window to escape. This closes a loop for the audience: *"So that's what the heavy box was for!"*

Using previously established objects to solve a problem is much more powerful—and easier—than creating a new solution. These are the moments of genius where nobody believes you didn't script the scene in advance. By paying attention to the environment, you can find these genius moments more often.

Find New Ideas

Reincorporation is just one example of the biggest benefit of environment work: it helps you generate ideas for *anything* you need.

Every improviser hears this in one form or another: *"When you're stuck, turn to the environment." "Find an object, or begin an activity, and you'll find a way to link it to the scene."* But really, just wave your hands around a space object and the Universe will deliver a working scene? It sounds like magic, or some manifestation of *The Secret*. Rarely does anyone talk about *why* this works and how to do it reliably.

My bold claim is this: *Become proficient with physical improv and you will never be at a loss for what to do next.* All the "advanced" elements of scene work—character, narrative, Game of the scene, and so on—are easily inspired by ideas from the environment.

How? It's no Secret. I can give you the one-line version right now: *by noting your own physicality and building ideas on top of it.* I'll show you this process in Part III, and in Part IV I'll give you tips for inspiring specific scene elements if you need them.

Your First Thought Experiment

To begin understanding how you can get ideas from environment work, let's consider an example. Keep in mind we're talking about improv—any scene can go in any direction at any time. The example scenes I describe throughout this book are thought experiments. They're only meant to show how you might free-associate through possible options. I'm not declaring a definitive way you should do things on stage. Think alongside me and see what ideas you might come up with in the same situation.

I like to perform these experiments when I find myself in unusual places. As it happens, I'm writing this passage of the book while on an airplane, so that seems as good a place as any to start. What could you do with the suggestion of "an airplane" as the location for a scene?

Whenever you get a generic suggestion, you might first think about *specificity*. What type of airplane is it? An Airbus? A biplane? A cargo jet? A military transport? Maybe it's one of those coin-operated airplane rides you see at the mall. Each of these generates different ideas for what might happen in that place.

Then there are possible *sub-locations* for an airplane. Are you in the cockpit? Waiting outside the lavatory? On the wing? Maybe you're a baggage handler stowing luggage. Even the passenger cabin can have sub-locations—are you in First Class or Coach?[4]

As you consider each of these, is your mind drifting toward possible story ideas? This is the power of a specific location.

Now, since I'm sitting in Coach as I write this, let's go with that. At the moment, they've interrupted our dinner service because of some rough weather turbulence. I'm typing with one hand while keeping my drink from spilling with the other. That's a good start for a scene!

But think of all the detail that the last paragraph skips over. Is it mild turbulence, or is the plane really shaking? Are you holding a glass of water, or red wine? Or steaming hot coffee that's sloshing everywhere? Or tequila, if you're really freaking out?

Who is sitting nearby? What time of day is it? Is the seat comfortable, or is the guy in front of you reclining into your knees? The answers are all environmental choices. Each can send the scene off into so many different directions. Thinking this way generates a ton of inspiring ideas, and the great thing is *you only need ONE to get started.* If the scene drags, or you get stuck for an idea, you can always return to the environment for more inspiration.

You can choose to indulge your sense of play in this scene. You could constantly vibrate your body because of the turbulence. You could spill hot coffee on yourself or other characters. You could get thrown out of your seat, or right out the window!

You can also choose to dig deeper into character, relationship, or narrative. Is there a difference in behavior between people in First Class vs. Coach? Are you and your boss fighting over the armrest? How might the turbulence put an interesting edge on any conflict in the scene?

Now, these thought experiments are one thing, but you're likely still wondering how to actually do all this on the stage. The good news is, you can practice the skills not only to make these choices more instinctively but also to act them out in ways that bring people right into the airplane with you.

And that's what the rest of this book is about.

---

[4] I regularly use *Sub-Locations* as an exercise in my workshops. You'll find a description in the Appendix on page 185.

2

First Principles

Chapter Outline

Most improvisation manuals take a broad overview of spontaneous storytelling. My concern with this book is that, by going deep into one topic, readers will come to overvalue environment work. But no one improv skill is more important than the others, and every improviser benefits from a well-rounded set of tools. As we get started, let me put this work into a larger context and clarify a few other basic points.

Definitions

"Physical Improv"

In *physical theatre*, movement and physicality are the primary mode of storytelling. When I refer to *physical improv*, I use a broader definition. It's *any* technique that creates an illusion of physical objects, activities, and locations that aren't really there. In some situations, even dialogue or emotional reactions can do this. For example, shuddering in terror as you describe a tornado bearing down on you is a perfectly legitimate example of physical improv.

"Scene"

When I talk about performing in a *scene*, I mean any type of improvised story you're telling, in whatever format. Physical improv works for long-form and short-form, solo and group work, games and open scenes.

Improv Terms

For new improvisers still learning our vocabulary, I've included a *Glossary of Improv Terms* at the end of the book. If I've missed something, you can easily find other glossaries online. Be aware that sometimes there is regional variation and even some disagreement over definitions.

Tools not Rules

If it didn't make the book harder to read, I would have asked my publisher to stamp those three words on every page. The techniques in this book have worked tremendously well for me, but they're not rigid methods to be applied in every situation. If you treat them that way, they can actually wreck your scenes.

Improv is always uncertain, and it's natural to want a predictable method for generating a result. However, I'm skeptical of methods for two reasons. First, they can't possibly cover every situation. If you become too reliant on a method, you may panic when it suddenly doesn't work. Second, because a method always uses the same steps, it will tend to generate similar results. You'll eventually become bored by the lack of variety in your improv. (And so will the audience.)

Everything in this book is a tool, ready for you to use in any situation. For good results, though, you have to practice using tools to know when they work and when they don't. Some tools won't work at all for you. That's okay, too. Try everything, keep what works, and discard the rest.

Let me also add to the growing calls for an end to the teaching of improv "rules," such as *"Don't ask questions"* or *"Don't do teaching scenes."* In her book *Improvise Freely*, Patti Stiles writes that rules restrict behavior, which kills your creativity. Rules can also be used to justify dangerous behavior that risks hurting performers physically or emotionally. Most of the rules handed down to improvisers are at best guidelines. Instructors use them to help beginners stay out of trouble and set them up for successful outcomes during their basic training. But I firmly believe that, as long as you're playing with skill and respect, it's possible to make *any* type of improv scene work.

I feel the same way about the debate over one improv style being "better" than others. Defining yourself according to one approach is as creatively limiting as any improv rule. Luckily, physical improv is available for players of any style.

Not Every Scene Needs a Where

Many of my students get caught in the belief that they have to be more physical in *every scene, all the time*. That's not the case. In fact, if you focus too much on the Where, it's possible to lose the most important elements of any given scene. And sometimes, *not* going to the Where can be a powerful choice.

Most conventionally told stories do have a clear Who/What/Where platform. But there are other ways to tell a story. Sometimes you may want to put the audience off-balance, which is easy to do if you withhold information. A dream sequence, for example, seems to always start with someone saying *"Where am I?"* and getting no answer.

You can also delay establishing the Where until later in the scene. The audience often assumes a location from the characters, dialogue, and story events they see. Revealing somewhere different creates a startling turn that can redirect the scene. An example is the classic reframe where two nuns have a serious conversation before a bartender appears to serve their martinis. Reframes are often cheap gags, but they're definitely an option.

Again, this is about knowing your tools. Study how authors withhold information for narrative effect. Research different theatre, book, film, and TV styles and genres. Resolve to tell your stories in different ways beyond the Who/What/Where standard.

Prioritize Characters over Objects

There are always exceptions, but an improvised story is hardly ever about the *thing* you're doing. It's about how the characters experience that thing, either to achieve an objective or to express an emotion. The best stories have characters with a strong point of view that motivates their actions. Environment is just one of many filters through which characters can express their point of view. Physical improv effects are most powerful when they reveal character.

Consider a scene set in an office. As you go, you can interact with many objects. You might sit at a desk, type on a computer, pour yourself a coffee, search through a file cabinet, and so on. This does provide a sense of place, but if there's no real point to the activity, the story doesn't move forward. At a certain point it becomes distracting.

Now, suppose you're playing a lazy assistant trying to look busy, or a panicky accountant searching for a lost document. For these characters, all that activity would be natural and expected. By linking it back to the emotions and motivations of the character, you can play with the environment all day. And the audience will be happy to watch.

Of course, you *can* add objects for color's sake—sometimes a coffee cup is only a coffee cup. But it's usually better to show us one object that connects to the character than spend the whole scene filtering through random stuff.

Play with Your Partners

Whether reading a book or taking classes, learning physical improv is frequently a solitary activity. There are many solo exercises, as every player must practice with their own body and level of capability. Even in performance, your character will often do a separate activity while others do their thing. Never forget that *you are all working together* to create the world of your scene. Give and take is extremely important to maintaining an improvised reality. Keep track of what your partners do, so you can give their environment work the same care and attention you give your own.

Be careful not to get distracted by your own object work. It's possible to go so deep and detailed that your attention gets pulled away from your partners, and the character interactions get lost. This is especially a concern if you're in the background while others are having a conversation.

Avoid unintentionally *pulling focus*. Movement attracts the eye, which means your environment work can easily distract other players and the audience. To keep the focus on the scene's primary characters and events, you must always be aware of distraction, and be ready to dial back your physicality.

Note that it's easy to deliberately pull focus through odd behavior in the background, and sometimes that adds a bit of fun if everyone is ready to play. But excessive gagging kills scenes and doesn't make you much fun to play with.

A third issue is making sure your partners can always see your object work, so they observe and understand your offers. Sometimes characters keep their behavior secret—while they're nearby, you could be penning an anonymous love letter or poisoning their drink. Your partner's *character* may not know this, but the *improviser* needs to know. Don't hide it away from them. By practicing stage presence, you will learn how to watch your partners while maintaining the illusion that the character is oblivious to what's going on.

Safety First, Last, and Always

Despite my earlier thoughts about rules in improv (i.e., there really aren't any), one principle we must all understand is *the need to play safely*. Especially with physical improv, there are a lot of ways you can injure yourself or others, physically or emotionally. If you only read one section of this book, I'd very much prefer you read Part V, all about safety.

Part II

Object Work

One of Viola Spolin's keenest insights was that *we know where we are by the objects around us*. Even if you've never been there before, you know you're in a kitchen because there are food-preparation tools there. You know you're in a factory because of the manufacturing machinery. And so on. I'm sure there are exceptions to this principle, but it's a good basis for our work in improvisation.

Object work is your primary tool as an improv illusionist. It's also called *mime*, but most improvisers avoid that term. Maybe it's because mime implies a formal study and practice that performers find hard to live up to (and which is unnecessary for improv). Or maybe they just don't like mimes.

You Will Learn

- how reproducing object details helps the audience "see" things that aren't there;
- the basics of using your hands, body, and movement to create the illusion of objects;
- to think in routines, which adds clarity and detail to your activities; and
- common bad habits of object work and how to avoid them.

3

Making the Invisible Visible

Sometime around 1983, I saw my first sketch and improv revue at The Second City in Toronto. It was very different from other plays I had seen. The Old Firehall Theatre was a dark and cramped cabaret. The back wall was painted off-white, with a curtained arch on one side and a dutch door on the other. Apart from a couple of black, bentwood chairs, the stage was empty. Even then it seemed impossibly small for a cast of six actors.

Early in the show, there was a scene with two lovers in a studio apartment. One of the actors began to mime opening a bottle of wine. For a moment, it was seriously weird. Why weren't they using props? Where was the set?

I was only unbalanced for a moment, though, because I quickly realized the props and set weren't necessary. I could tell it was a wine bottle and a corkscrew. I knew the bentwood chairs they were sitting on were a cozy loveseat. From the way the woman looked into the corner, there was clearly a bed waiting. The actors were simply behaving as if everything was there. And to my surprise, *I felt like I could see it.*

This is the genius of object work. You can take a story anywhere, instantly, without having to gather props or change the set. Object work transports the audience into your scene. As long as you do it well.

Good object work is important because the audience (and your scene partners) can't read your mind. *You* know exactly what object you're holding and what you're doing with it, but everyone else has to read your movements to understand. The curve of your fingers shows them whether you're holding a beer bottle or a coffee mug. The turn of your wrist and the swing of your arm shows them whether you're opening a door or swinging a sword.

Clear, specific detail is the key. You don't have to study mime or take detailed movement training. You just have to be clear and specific about how you communicate information. Otherwise, you risk confusion.

Attitude

Before we get into understanding the physical elements of object work, we need to talk about the mental. This isn't a digression, it's an essential first step.

Before you move a muscle, your attitude is the crucial starting point. *You have to treat the objects as absolutely real.* I'm very passionate about this point, and you should be too.

When you improvise, you're inhabiting a character. In that character's world, the object is *there.* If they walk into the space where the table is, they will hit the table. It will hurt. They don't think twice about it.

If you the actor have the attitude of opening an "imaginary" wine bottle with a "pretend" corkscrew, you're working from inside your head, not embodying the character. This will affect your movements—they'll seem stiff and unnatural. Focus outward on the objects, as your character does, and your body will fall in line.

One common attitude issue is using your hand as an *indicator*, as if it's the actual object. For example, I've seen people use their index finger as a knife, spreading jam directly on their other hand, which is supposed to be a piece of toast. We've all seen people show guns with thumb straight up and index finger as the barrel. Or hold a phone by speaking into their pinky and listening to their thumb. These "shortcuts" are NOT object work.

You may wonder, *"What's the big deal?"* Everybody understands what you're doing, so that's successful communication, right?

Well, for one thing, if your hand is the object, you can't realistically manipulate it. If you're going to show us eating that toast, are you going to gnaw on your own hand? How will that look? Your storytelling draws the audience into a trance—indicator shortcuts knock them out of it.

One day, you may find yourself playing a threatening character, like a mob hitman. You'll enter the scene, and the other characters will cower before you. The audience will be on edge. Holding an improvised gun that has weight, with a finger that looks like it could squeeze the trigger any second, can be as terrifying as the real thing. If everyone commits to the reality of the object, the audience believes it. This makes you look like a genius actor.

Not so much if you pull out your finger gun. You can play that for a laugh, but there's no way you'll be able to continue a serious moment. It won't look right, and you'll lose your connection with the audience.

It's the same with the phone. Holding a believable handset, you can show us the anguish of someone breaking up with you on the other end of the line. That moment doesn't ring true if it looks like you're holding a banana to your ear. Improv is more than just disposable theatre. If you want to tell memorable stories, your performance attitude matters.

A classic Viola Spolin exercise asks you to treat space as a real substance that can be felt and manipulated. Improvised objects take shape as if you're molding this substance like clay. Some people find this weird. But working with *"space stuff"* gives you outward focus and body involvement that makes your object work seem more real, as opposed to standing there waving your arms mechanically.

Space Substance/Space Shaping

Working solo, players stand with palms facing each other, moving hands closer together and further apart, focusing on the space between. This is not rigid, aimless hand-waving. Really try to feel the "space stuff" between your hands.

Next, try working with a partner to sense the space substance between you. You can also explore moving through space, feeling it with your whole body.

> Once you have some experience with space substance, try shaping it with your hands, arms, and body. Allow it to take shape as an object, if it does, but don't force it.

This is where the term *space object* comes from. To reinforce the proper attitude, we use this term instead of *pretend object* or *imaginary object.*

Some instructors (including Spolin) coach you to *"see"* the object as you work with it. If you can do this easily, great. I find it difficult, and I've learned that many people feel the same. I don't feel you have to hold an image in your mind for good object work.[1] But making an effort to experience the object in some way does help with body involvement.

In any case, treating the object as real is a necessary starting point.

The Science of Mime

So, how does the improv illusion actually work? Why does moving your hands in certain ways cause people to see you throwing a ball, or eating a sandwich?

There's actual scientific research into this, courtesy of Chaz Firestone, an assistant professor in the Department of Psychological and Brain Sciences at Johns Hopkins University. He's studied how the mind processes the "implied objects" created by mimes. In his study, he filmed himself colliding with an actual wall and stepping onto an actual box, then had those objects removed from the video so that he appeared to be miming these actions. After each of these clips, subjects were shown a black line, either horizontal or vertical, that matched or mismatched the orientation of the surface that had just been mimed. They were told to ignore the mime and just answer as quickly as possible if the line was horizontal or vertical. Firestone's team found people's answers were significantly faster when the orientation of the line aligned with the mimed wall or box. This suggests that they couldn't help seeing the mime, even if they were told to ignore it.[2]

---

[1] I'll talk more about visualization, and why it's unnecessary, in Chapter 7.
[2] For a deeper explanation of the experiment and its conclusions, check out the JHU News Release, which includes an interesting summary video. https://releases.jhu.edu/2021/04/01/mimes-help-us-see-objects-that-dont-exist/

I'm sorry if all that has your eyes glazed over. The one-sentence version is that mime appears to exploit a biological perception process—our brains "see" implied objects *automatically*. This is very good news, because it means there's no "secret trick" to mime. All you have to do is provide enough specific, recognizable detail to trigger recognition of the object. Once observers know what the object is, their brains will take over to create the illusion.

Your job is to understand how to communicate this detail, and know when to add more if needed.

Object Interactions

Let's think about Spolin's classic *Play Ball* exercise. Everyone understands how to "throw" and "catch" an improvised ball, so it's a good one for breaking this down.

Play Ball

Players stand in a circle and agree on a size/type of improvised ball, then toss it among themselves. Focus on consistency—keep the ball the same size, shape, and weight at all times. The coach can call out instructions to change the properties of the ball.

What do you notice about how people move with the ball, and how does this relate to "seeing" it?

In passing the ball around, most of us experience moments of feeling like we see a real ball. Something about the way a person moves connects to our visual senses. But what did they actually do?

The remarkable thing about mime is that you can never show the object itself—it's invisible and will always be so. It's your *interaction* with the object that reveals it. Here's a list of common characteristics of a ball and example interactions that communicate those details:

- **Shape.** I can balance any size ball on my open palm, but by curling my fingers or adding another hand, I show you how big it is.
- **Weight.** Even an inflatable beach ball has weight. By using different speed and effort in moving my arm, I can show how heavy the ball is.

- **Familiarity.** Even though it's possible to pass the ball in different ways, a familiar throwing action is easier to read than, say, bouncing it off my elbow.
- **Energy.** Intensity of motion. Think of how you might toss around a tennis ball vs. a priceless Fabergé egg. How would you throw and catch a burning hot coal?
- **Attitude.** How important is it to me that you successfully catch the ball? I could pause to make sure I have your attention. Or I could carelessly toss it without even making eye contact.
- **Direction.** The ball will travel in the direction I move.
- **Grasp and Release.** I close my hand around the ball to catch it. I open my hand to let it go. Release also connects to Direction—the position and angle of my hand when it opens indicates which way the ball travels.
- **Tracking.** I can track the ball movement with my head and eyes.
- **Consistency and Permanence.** Everyone handles the ball in the same way, and it doesn't change over time. If we put the ball down, we retrieve it from the same place later. This is how we agree with others' physical offers.

Most of these interactions are instinctive. You don't think of them when doing object work, and you don't have to. I'm just illustrating how much information our natural perception picks up. When you realize how much detail your movements provide, you can find ways of adding more to make improvised objects seem real.

Depending on the object, some interactions will be more powerful than others. Grasp and Release is a big one with the ball. If you don't open your hand, it doesn't matter how much you wave your arm. To the observer, you're still holding the ball.

Tiny details can easily trip up your object work. If your movements don't match our understanding of the common properties of an object, the illusion breaks. We may still understand the *concept* of what you're doing, but we don't *see* the object. Or sometimes we might see a different object than what you intend.

Notice how many interactions are related to movement of the arms and hands. These are our body's main tools for interacting with the world. As such, you can only communicate some details through your fine-motor mobility—curling your fingers a certain way, for example. This does make object work a challenge for improvisers with mobility issues, but it's not impossible. Interactions for Tracking and Energy don't require fine-motor skill but still contribute to the illusion. (In Chapter 8, we'll look at other less physical ways to show objects.)

If you struggle with object work, you *can* use this information to break down your movements and think about what's not working. However, there's a much easier, more natural way to practice interactions. And that is . . .

Muscle Memory

It seems obvious that, by studying the details of physical reality, you can reproduce them more easily in your object work. So how is it that we handle objects all day every day, but still have trouble when showing them through mime?

Most of the time, we don't think about the actions it takes to hold a physical object. Think about how you're holding this book right now (or the electronic device you may be reading it on). You curve your fingers a certain way. Small muscles in your hand and arm keep it from falling. Or maybe you're balancing it in your lap, which positions your legs a certain way. You tilt your head toward the book to read it. Your eyes move along these lines. You turn the pages with a specific combination of movements.

If I took the book from you right now, could you continue all this as if it was still there? Of course you could. You could remember how your body feels, and keep reproducing that. Paying attention to this *muscle memory* is all it takes to improve the clarity of your object work.

This is easy to practice.

Muscle Memory

Grab any small (real) object that's within reach. How does your arm move to pick it up? How do the fingers curl around it? Is it heavy or light? Do you have to grip it hard to lift, or do you have a light touch? Let go and notice the release. Pick it up and put it down a few times to notice how it feels. Try it with different speed and energy. Think about what changes and what stays the same.

Notice also that some objects have connected movements. When you drink from a cup, not only does your arm move, your lips do too, and so does your throat as you swallow. These connections are often the A-level specifics that create an illusion.

Now try those same motions again *without the object*. See how easy it is to reproduce the detail?

Another good tip is to try this in front of a mirror. Knowing what your movements look like to an outside observer helps train your performer's "third eye."

You can practice muscle memory all day long, with anything and everything you touch. Drinking coffee. Working at your computer. Putting on a sweater. Notice what the movements are, and then take a few seconds to repeat them without the object. It doesn't take much work or time to greatly improve your object handling.

Training Your Instinct

Clearly, you don't have to pick up every physical object in the universe to learn how to reproduce it in improv. The muscle memory technique is only a training tool—you don't use it on stage. We're developing your *instinct for movement*, which transfers to other objects you've never touched.

For example, chances are you've never wielded a two-handed battle ax. That doesn't mean you have to sit out of your improv scene if an orc fight breaks out. Your body already knows what it's like to pick up something large and heavy. It knows how your fingers curve around a long-handled object, like a broom or a baseball bat. And it knows how to balance yourself when swinging. You don't think about these things—you just pick up the ax and join the battle. Practicing with muscle memory trains these body instincts to work even better.

Instinct also pulls details from your memory and imagination. If you've seen *Lord of the Rings,* or *The Shining*, you've seen someone swing an ax. You must have seen someone chop wood at least once. What you've seen, you can reproduce, which is a good argument for gathering lots of life experience to support your improv.

Once you've worked with muscle memory for a bit, handling *any* space object is easy. Start with two things: *shape* and *weight*. Position your hands and body to show us the size of what you're holding, and how heavy it is. The rest falls into line if you follow your instinct for how your body would move with the real thing.

The following exercises help train your movement instincts:

Transformation of Objects

Players stand in a circle. Player 1 creates an object and passes it on. Player 2 transforms the object into something else, and so on. Players should receive and play with an object first, to discover a change instead of thinking one up and forcing it. Associations don't count either—creating a mirror to use with a comb isn't a transformation. Work with the motion of the previous object to help the transformation.

Object Toss

One of my favorite catch games. Players name any small object they can think of, and then toss it across the circle, for example, a hammer, a fried egg sandwich, a loose deck of cards, a goldfish in a bag. Try to keep the object consistent as you throw and catch. Once the receiving player catches the object, they call out a new one.

Let me emphasize why it's important to practice this. With body movement, there are two common dangers that instinct can lead you into. One is physical, the other is mental, and they can actually *hold back* your object work. Deliberate practice will help you spot these tendencies and control them.

Danger #1: Muscle Strains

Again, pick up a real object and focus on what your body does. Maybe take a drink from a coffee mug, or scroll through your phone.

The structure of your hand and body is imposed on you by the object. Your muscles react to its physical characteristics: solidity, weight, and so on. For example, with a real coffee mug, gravity puts more pressure on some fingers and less on others. Your body constantly makes tiny adjustments to relieve and distribute this pressure.

Take the object away and continue the activity. Notice that now you're working your muscles against *themselves*. To recreate the mug, you tense your fingers differently. And to maintain the illusion, you will tend to hold them fixed in place, often for a long time. Done to extremes, this creates a risk of injury.

Try this: imagine you're standing in front of a school bus. There's a heavy chain on the ground, tied to the front bumper. *VERY GENTLY*—pick up this improvised chain and pull on it like you're in one of those "strongest person" contests.

If you're working to make this look real, your body instinct may be to lean backward, tensing your arms. Or you might turn with the "chain" over your shoulder, leaning forward and pushing with your legs. You might even grimace with effort, tensing your face and neck. Be careful, don't overdo it! Put in only enough effort to feel the muscles contract. Look down and observe your arms and legs.

All of this creates an effective illusion. But because there's no heavy object there, you're tensing your muscles differently. It's very easy to strain yourself, especially when you add in the adrenaline of performing in front of an audience.

Contracting your muscles isn't necessary. Try holding the same position of pulling the bus, and then release as much tension as you can. Just pose yourself and feel your muscles relax. Now see if you can continue to move forward slowly without added tension.

To an observer, your posture shows the effort. We can easily see you're pulling something. Within a scene, we'd also have the context of knowing what you're pulling. The only muscle contraction necessary is what it takes to hold that posture, which isn't much at all.

Important Safety Tip: Avoid Muscle Strains!

Only a small amount of body tension is necessary to hold the posture for an object. When practicing, try holding the shape of the object and then releasing your muscles as much as possible. Carry this practice into your improv onstage. *Remind yourself to relax.*

Be especially mindful of facial grimaces or grunted dialogue. They help show effort, but the muscles in your face and neck can be very delicate. Avoid holding your breath, which also puts stress on your body.

This is NOT something you will do easily on your first try, especially in the middle of an improv show. You're fighting the natural instinct to tense your muscles. Practice offstage with various postures and movements so you can learn to release muscle tension.

You'll notice I'm very big on performer safety. There's a whole chapter with more tips in Part V of this book.

At the Gym

A good exercise for muscle memory practice. Show us how you might lift weights at the gym without physically tensing your muscles. Try different weights, types, and sizes. Are you using free weights or machines? Be careful not to "lift" too much—protect yourself from injury!

Danger #2: Grooves

Throughout this book, I'm going to remind you of an essential concept: VARIETY. We always want our improv to be on the edge of the unknown, the unpredictable. Patterns of behavior are dangerous because they kill spontaneity. Repetition quickly becomes boring for audiences. It also hurts your scene work, because predictability can easily cause you to check out of a scene and lose focus.

The problem is, our brains *love* patterns and repetition. They give us safety, which we're wired to seek out. Your natural instincts will constantly fall into repeating behavior, like a needle falling into a record groove. For variety in your improv, you need to be aware of this and work against it.

This is especially true for object work. You may drink from the same type of coffee mug all the time. Or, when looking to add a bit of stage business, you may default to the same activity.

Technically, there's nothing wrong with this. But when your actions are in a groove, your thinking tends to follow. You may notice yourself creating the same types of scenes over and over. Or worse, the audience may notice. New, spontaneous ideas come to you when you work in a state of uncertainty. Varying up your activity helps keep you in that state.

You can fight the groove by deliberately practicing with muscle memory. Play with objects in different ways. Make them slightly larger, or heavier, or add strange shapes or details to them.

This makes your object work much more flexible. You'll be more aware of details and be able to switch them up.

Begin and End with Objects

Here's another classic Viola Spolin exercise for learning to work with space objects. It's a slower, more exacting version of the basic muscle memory technique. It helps to have observers to tell you what they see, but you can also try it on your own. Consider filming yourself and studying the playback.

Begin and End with Objects

1. Decide on a small improvised object with a simple action, for example, buttering a slice of toast, opening a pickle jar, pouring a glass of milk. Perform this without any modification.
2. Repeat the action again, one single movement at a time. At the beginning of each movement, call *"Begin!"* When finished that movement, call *"End!"* Take your time—there's no rush. With the pickle jar example, it might go like this:

   - *"Begin!"* Reach out and grab the jar. *"End!"*
   - *"Begin!"* Pick up the jar. *"End!"*
   - *"Begin!"* Move your other hand to the lid. *"End!"*
   - *"Begin!"* Twist your hand on the lid. *"End!"*
   - *"Begin!"* Open your hand and reset. *"End!"*
   - *"Begin!"* Twist again. *"End!"*
   - *"Begin!"* Pull the lid off. *"End!"*
   - *"Begin!"* Put the lid down. *"End!"*
   - *"Begin!"* Reach into the jar and grab a pickle. *"End!"*
   - *"Begin!"* Pull the pickle out. *"End!"*

3. Repeat the whole action a third time, as fast as possible and without calling out. Observers usually notice a sharper, more visible object compared to the first time. You may find you're able to see it more clearly as well.

Call out *"Begin!"* and *"End!"* each time with energy and volume—this helps you get out of your head and into your body. And take it slow. You're breaking the specific movements down, making each one deliberate.

Coaches and observers: When evaluating, comment on what you see, not the "correctness" of the individual movements. What's the actual visual effect of the action?

This exercise is a bit of a mind-bender the first few times you try it. It can be hard to get the rhythm. Stick with it. It's a brain habit to want to execute an action as one continuous event. If you feel resistance in this exercise, it's because you're forcing yourself to break down the action into individual details. This is exactly what we want!

You can also try this exercise with actual physical objects to build your muscle memory.

Trouble

Life doesn't always go smoothly. When telling stories through improv, you have to let your characters fail sometimes. It humanizes them and creates new story opportunities.

We can extend this thinking to simple object work. A technique that makes things seem more real is *Trouble*.

Clothing provides lots of examples. Imagine putting on a pair of oversized coveralls. The material will flop around a bit, but it's easy to step into them and zip them up. Now think of a tight, neoprene wet suit. Your legs and arms will stick inside it, and you have to tug it on. Even wearing your favorite old sweatshirt is rarely a simple process.

Clothing Trouble

Choose various types of improvised clothes. Practice putting them on or taking them off. Look for small "trouble" details like pulling on fabric or working with zippers and buttons.

Every object has little "trouble moves" like these. They're so common, we barely notice them. But they add huge levels of detail to your object work. When putting on a pair of glasses, what if you notice and polish a smudge on the lens first? What if they slide down your nose and you push them up with your finger? These moves give life to your improvised props.

Some objects have trouble built into their use which is necessary to show. When you're chopping down a tree, the ax will get stuck in the wood at least some of the time. If you don't show that, your object work will look like you're pounding on the tree with a sledgehammer.

Trouble can provide "business" for your character when the focus of a scene is on other characters. It keeps you from standing still, which looks unnatural. In the background, you can always find an object nearby to fiddle with. However, be careful not to pull focus from your scene partners—it's easy to do.[3]

You can also express unique character traits through trouble. The way a teenager dons a pair of skinny jeans is different than for an eighty-year-old. For the senior citizen, that could be a whole scene!

Problems with objects don't always happen, and they don't *have* to happen. Trouble isn't something you should use all the time, especially if it's distracting to you or the audience. Less is more.

Here are some exercises to help you practice:

Difficulty with Small Objects

A single player becomes involved with a small object or a piece of clothing, for example, opening a pill bottle, fixing a stuck zipper. This can be expanded to involve two or more players working together.

Focused Work

A variation on *Difficulty with Small Objects*. A single player chooses and performs an activity with small objects and very fine detail, for example, needlepoint, painting tiny figurines, building a model airplane. Maintain this activity while carrying on a conversation, with the coach or another player working separately.

Coaches: Watch for repetition or loss of detail, which are hints the player is losing focus.

---

[3] More so than with real props, audiences easily become fascinated by improvised business. Maybe they think that since you're doing something deliberate, it might be important to the scene. Whatever the reason, it's another example of how powerful object work can be.

Trapped

A single player chooses a small, contained environment from which to escape, for example, a bear trap, a stuck elevator. For added challenge, you could add a character element. How might a mouse escape from a mousetrap?

Coaches: Be careful with this one—players will often strain themselves trying to pull free, which can cause injury. Learn to show effort without physically tensing the muscles.

Object Work in Performance

When you eventually get on stage, it will be time to leave all the practice behind and just do the object work. Your focus will be to keep things clear and specific, so the audience and your partners can read you. Here are a few thoughts to keep in mind. As always, there are no hard-and-fast rules.

- **Remember the First Principles.** Prioritize characters over objects. Play with your partners. Safety first, last, and always. (Revisit Chapter 2.)
- **Less is more.** Let objects emerge organically as needed rather than actively filling the scene with them. This also makes it easier to remember where everything is.
- **Be specific.** Make a clear choice about what the object is. Your character may desperately want "a drink," but what are you drinking? Your hands and body will need to do things differently if you're downing a shot of whiskey or sipping a milkshake.
- **Face the audience.** Your instinct may be to put large objects like filing cabinets or artwork against the back wall. Instead, work with them out front, where everyone can see you. If it's a really large object, you can think of it as being in the audience space, with its edge against the front of the stage.
- **Avoid mixing real and space objects.** I see this happen a lot with clothing, where a player chooses to take off their real shoes, then later takes off an improvised jacket. Whatever effect you might achieve with a real prop is lost to confusion when you start improvising other objects. I think you're better to always improvise every object, but you should at least stay consistent if you introduce real props.

- **Use other people's objects.** Reusing an idea is easier than coming up with your own. Respect object permanence—watch where your partners set up objects and furniture, then use them the same way. The audience really appreciates improvisers working together.

"But It Feels Weird . . ."

Improvisers often avoid object work because it feels unnatural. You may experience this even more when practicing by yourself than when you do it onstage.

Here's the thing: *it DOES feel unnatural!*

Spoiler Alert: You're not actually holding anything. You're just moving your body and pretending. Of course it's going to feel weird. I've been swinging space axes and drinking from space mugs for twenty-five years. It's never once felt "natural." If you feel awkward doing it, be confident that you're not broken.

The audience understands object work. If you do it with a little skill, they don't think twice about it. With a little practice, you build that skill and gain confidence. But you *do* have to practice. Don't worry—it won't take long before it becomes second nature.

For More About Mime

As far as I'm concerned, those are the basics of handling objects. Professional mime training can no doubt teach you a lot more, including specific techniques like "popping," where you add a tiny bit of extra energy to the beginning and end of your movements. This and other mime instruction brings much higher levels of precision to your object work. For most types of improv, though, none of it is necessary.

One resource I will mention is a small chapter in Tom Salinsky and Deborah Frances-White's *The Improv Handbook*, titled (funnily enough) "You Can't Learn Mime from a Book." Of all the improv books in my library, this is the best writing on object work I've been able to find. (And it includes a section about "popping.") Too bad it's only six pages.

Now, there's more to life than picking things up and putting them down. Let's talk about how we can make our improvised activities seem more real.

4

Activities and Routines

One big factor in helping people see space objects is *familiarity*. It's easier for an observer to read what you're doing if your movements fit their experience. This might seem obvious, but it's powerful. The most precise object work can become confusing if it doesn't match what people expect to see.

This is even more important when moving from single objects to activities. An activity has a series of routine steps, specific movements that occur one after the other. If you miss showing a step, or it's not made clear, the observer can lose track and become confused.

To prevent this, it's useful to spend time thinking through these *routines*.[1] Just like muscle memory for objects, routines train your instinct for improvising activities.

Avoid the Void

First, another brief note about your attitude toward object work. In improv, you create the world, revealing location and objects as you go through the

---

[1] In *Impro for Storytellers*, Keith Johnstone describes *anything* the characters are doing as a routine. I use the term more specifically, to break down the physical steps of an activity.

scene. To your character, though, the world isn't a formless Void that slowly becomes visible. Things don't just appear out of thin air—they've been there the whole time.

In the middle of a scene, wanting to make something happen, there's a strong instinct to just grab an object and go with it. But where did that object come from? If it was there the whole time, it must have been resting on a piece of furniture, or leaning against something else. When you snatch it out of the Void, you deny that reality, especially if you've already walked through that space beforehand, or do so moments later. (I'll talk more about this in Chapter 5.)

Whenever you start an activity routine, take a moment to clarify the space for yourself and the audience. Locate and retrieve the objects you need rather than grabbing them out of nothing.

Thinking in Routines

Imagine a scene opening with a character brushing their teeth. Seems like a fairly common activity, easily performed. If the improviser rushes through it, though, we might see them do something like this:

- grab toothbrush (from the Void);
- squeeze toothpaste on it (where did that toothpaste tube come from?);
- brush teeth (likely with a few back-and-forth hand waves);
- spit; and
- drop brush (back into the Void).

It's possible to get away with this, of course. With a minimum of detail, everyone can still understand what's happening, and the scene will proceed. But apart from the risk that this doesn't happen, it looks unnatural and it feels rushed. Both the audience and the improviser lose a deeper level of involvement.

What's the *reality* of brushing your teeth? Picture how you do it in your own home. What are the actual steps you take? Here's my personal tooth-brushing routine. (I'm revealing my most intimate secrets because I really care about you.)

- pick up toothbrush handle from the charging stand (it's an electric—notice the *specificity*);
- pick up the brush head and stick it on the handle;
- turn on water faucet and wet the bristles;
- pick up the toothpaste tube;

- remove the toothpaste cap;
- squeeze toothpaste onto the brush;
- put the cap back on the tube and put the tube away (not being lazy);
- put the brush in my mouth and turn it on;
- press the secondary speed button to dial it down a bit (I have sensitive gums);
- brush one quadrant for thirty seconds (the brush has a beeping timer);
- brush second quadrant for thirty seconds;
- brush third quadrant for thirty seconds (sigh);
- brush fourth quadrant for thirty seconds (and feel superior about my good oral hygiene);
- turn off brush (or else it sprays everywhere);
- spit;
- rinse brush under the water;
- rinse my mouth and face;
- towel off face and brush;
- pull the brush head off and put it away; and
- put the handle back on the charging stand.

Note that I could extend this routine by including earlier steps, such as entering the bathroom and turning on the light. I could also add more steps to the end, or chain this to another routine, such as flossing. And I could break some of those steps down even more—for example, I might take the towel off its rack and return it later.

Even the simplest activities generate a list like this. See how much detail you sacrifice when you rush?

To train this, you can apply Viola Spolin's *Begin-and-End* exercise (from the last chapter) to routines, the same way you do it with single objects. Each step and related movement of a routine has a beginning and an ending. Call these out as you do the activity and it may help you break things down more easily.

Another way to practice thinking in routines is to use the *What's Next?* exercise.

What's Next?

Single player or a group of players working separately. Choose an activity that takes more than a few steps to accomplish, for example, making a sandwich, loading a laundry machine. The coach or observers call out a first step, which player performs any way they interpret. Then the coach calls *"What's Next?"* to get a next step, and so on. Note how people approach activities in different ways—one person's next step may not be the same as another's. Have the players use the suggestions from the audience instead of their own ideas—it helps them see things differently.

When performing activities, asking yourself *"What's Next?"* helps you to slow down and focus on the detail.

The Benefits

You might be thinking, *"OMG, do you really do ALL those tooth-brushing steps on stage?"* Well, yes! It isn't something I have to remember how to do. I already do it twice a day for real, and can reproduce it easily thanks to muscle memory practice.

Performing the routine doesn't take much more time than the previous rushed version. By slowing down a tiny bit and adding more detail, I've given the audience something much more watchable. If brushing their teeth is important to this character, let's see them brushing their teeth, not an actor pretending!

The added detail also gives me more raw idea material to work with in my improv, as we'll talk about shortly.

On stage, I'd probably abbreviate brushing all four quadrants for thirty seconds each, but I don't have to. The boredom of brushing your teeth for a long time is something we can all relate to. I can choose to lean into this for laughs or to set my character up as a stickler for procedures. These ideas and choices might never come to mind if I don't think about the steps.

There are two other practical benefits to thinking in routines:

1. **You remember where you are.** More than likely, something in the scene will happen that interrupts your activity. Afterward, you'll need to pick up where you left off. Having a routine in mind makes it easier to return to the same place.
2. **You avoid mindless repetition.** Usually we do activities while talking about something else. As you focus on the dialogue, the activity might drop or turn into a repetitive motion that looks

unnatural. A routine keeps the activity flowing from one detailed step to the next.

Activity Trouble

As with basic object work, you can add *trouble* to play around with activities. Remember that trouble is anything that keeps an activity from going 100 percent smoothly. It can arise at any step of a routine, and dealing with it forces you to change your pace and energy.

Imagine a scene where you're escaping a sinking ship, and you've jumped into a lifeboat. One activity here might be taking out your pocket knife and cutting the rope to release the boat. Take a moment to think what the routine steps might be. Then, think about how you could add minor or major trouble to different steps in that routine. Some ideas:

- You check many pockets looking for the knife.
- The knife is rusty and hard to open.
- The knife isn't very sharp, which makes it tough to cut the rope.
- The knife is *too* sharp. You slash through the rope, but the knife falls and cuts a hole in the boat.
- You can't find a knife at all and have to use something else.

Activity trouble injects play into your improv. I love to add some when other characters are impatient or trying to hurry the situation. It slows things down and frustrates the hell out of them, which makes for some funny dynamics.

Breaking Routines

When trouble gets really bad, it *breaks the routine.* Depending on the scene, the consequences can be mild or severe. But it usually means you have to stop the activity and find something different to do.

If a scene seems to be going nowhere, often it's because your character hasn't got a clear objective. Breaking a routine can create a problem for you to fix, and this goal gives the scene a new direction. The classic pattern for this is breaking the routine at the exact moment your characters need it to work. The boss is coming over for dinner, but you've burned the pot roast. You need to bury the body, but the ground is frozen and the shovel breaks.

You're writing a paragraph about breaking routines and can't think of a third example. You get the idea.

Routines don't always have to break in extreme ways. I'm sure you're as bored as I am with improvisers using a kitchen knife and then gushing blood from a severed finger. Scenes like this are almost never played realistically and turn into frantic shouting. A smaller, simpler idea can be just as good, if not better. Maybe you run out of ingredients for the meal and have to find a creative substitute.

Scenes where *everything* goes wrong can be a lot of fun! Most of the great silent comedy actors have used this technique. All it takes is thinking about the routine and looking for ways to break each step. Start small and slowly make the consequences bigger.

One warning about breaking routines too often is that it keeps a scene from advancing. Be careful of *bridging*, where you delay doing or saying something that could clearly be done immediately. It sometimes works to create tension or suspense, but more often makes the scene boring. The audience jumps ahead of you and gets frustrated while they wait for you to catch up. Bridging is often caused by fear, when you don't know where you'll go once you've completed the activity. Maybe you should just do the thing and explore what comes next! With trouble and breaking routines, make it a deliberate choice and not a stalling tactic.

In fact, you can change up a routine without even finding a problem. You can simply have a reaction to what you're doing. Are you pleased with how it's going or are you becoming frustrated? Do you have a sudden thought that makes you want to speed up or slow down?

Breaking Routines

The player chooses and practices an activity routine, which they then perform without incident. Repeat the routine, but this time find two ways to break it (i.e., things go wrong). The first break is minor—they can fix or ignore it and continue. The second break is catastrophic and ends the activity.

For fun, you can do this as a Die game—the second break kills the character somehow. Encourage players to avoid the obvious choice, like stabbing themselves while cutting vegetables. (I don't recommend you use this variation when working with children. They will often make an extreme choice at the expense of the exercise and risk hurting themselves.)

Bad Habits

One day, in my Level 1 improv class at The Second City, our instructor Jerry Schaefer was teaching us how to set up a scene. For the first few weeks, our class had been doing basic object work, establishing locations by each contributing one object at a time. I really enjoyed it and had some early success, so of course I thought I knew everything.

I was wrong.

This exercise was our first time having a single player set up a location for others to join. My group's suggestion was "a reunion," and getting the idea for a family dinner, I stepped forward.

Jerry encouraged us to make quick assumptions. I decided this was a ritzy family, gathering around a grand dining table to sip dry gin and throw drier insults. As the person laying the table, that would make me the butler. So, with focused air and stiff resolve, I began my object work. (Yes, these are clichés. I was brand new at this.)

What a marvelous table it was! From a wheeled cart, I laid out fine china and silverware, crystal glasses, candles, even chafing dishes. I wasn't sure what a chafing dish was, but I knew there were a few on this table.

However, something was wrong. No one was joining me in the scene.

Looking back from years of experience, I know how to handle a situation like this. I might show a little more of my character, call to someone offstage, make eye contact with a nearby player, or even do the scene by myself. At that time, just starting out, I didn't know what to do. So I continued laying the table, waiting for a partner.

Four place settings became six, then ten, then twelve. I added water glasses, soup spoons, fish forks. There have been dining scenes in *Downton Abbey* with less hardware. All from a miraculously tiny cart. At least two minutes had gone by and still no one entered.

For the first time, I felt the yawning pit of despair that opens inside you when a scene goes wrong. But I was locked in. I was the butler, and it was my job to lay the table, so I kept going.

Finally, Jerry called it. I was still alone. All my "scene partners" shrugged their shoulders. One of them said, "I'm sorry. I couldn't figure out what you were doing." As beginners themselves, no one felt able to enter until they knew what was going on. None of the students in the audience could figure it out either.

I explained all I'd done, right down to the chafing dishes. Very politely, Jerry pointed out what he and everyone else actually saw. Not only had I walked through the space where I'd established the table *several times*, I had also placed every object in *exactly the same tiny area*. In my mind, I saw a massive piece of furniture, but in real space, I hadn't moved more than a few inches to put everything on it. Had they been real props, the table's contents would have been piled in one spot, all the way to the ceiling.

Only a few weeks into my training, I'd already internalized some bad habits. It stings to have them pointed out to you, but you can't overcome them otherwise.

Bad habits are signs you're too much in your head. You lose *presence* with the activity, which causes you to miss showing important details. Or, you lose *body involvement* and your movements don't seem authentic. Either way, people read you incorrectly. At best, it looks messy and artificial. At worst, no one can tell what you're doing.

It's easy to downplay the importance of this. After all, object work IS artificial and everyone knows it, so who cares how it looks? But when you hold the power to make people see what you want them to see, why give them the chance to see anything else? If you want to consistently captivate audiences, you need to hold your improv to a high standard. So, let's look at some common negative behaviors that crop up in object work, and how to avoid them.

Low Affect

I've mentioned attitude in the last two chapters, pointing out the importance of treating space objects as real and avoiding the instinct to grab them from "the Void." Even if you follow those two principles, there's a third attitude-related issue to watch out for—not being *affected* by the environment.

If the objects and conditions in a scene are real to the characters, then those things have *meaning*, too. Skilled object work seems hollow if we don't see that meaning. Imagine a bomb disposal scene where no one fears an explosion, an Arctic scene where no one feels the cold, an art gallery scene where precious sculptures are trashed and no one bats an eye. Even with incredible detail, low affect makes it seem like you're still playacting.

And then there's the trouble with guns. They're everywhere in our movies, TV, and video games, so much so that our reactions have become almost normalized. When a gun appears in an improv scene, it's almost never played realistically. Things usually devolve into a boring shouting match as characters fight for control.[1] If the gun goes off, characters barely react, especially the one who's been shot.

It's not that you must have a *specific* reaction to certain objects—that leads to clichéd melodrama. Not everyone cowers before a gun, for example. A soldier might be far more calm. Or, in your nervousness, you might do something unexpected, like start giggling. You may even choose to become "dead inside," which seems like you have low affect but which is actually an extreme reaction to a dangerous situation.

What I mean is, where an object or conditions would clearly affect the characters, you have to show us *something*. Unless you're playing it as a deliberate choice, low affect cuts you off from showing us a deeper experience.

Rooting

When we're focused on something mentally taxing, body movement is often suppressed. Evolutionary psychology explains this as a defense mechanism. In the wild, if you're not focused on protecting yourself from predators, it makes sense to not move around attracting attention.

---

[1] Often a gun appears because the *improviser* wants to control the scene, in reaction to fear and uncertainty. This is very common with beginners, especially kids.

This can happen when players become very focused on *improvising*. Even though you may be doing great object work with your hands and arms, your body may be "rooted" to the same place on stage. This was the problem in my butler scene—in my mind I was moving around the large table, but in reality I was barely moving at all.

Rooting is an unconscious behavior, like the swaying or shifting often seen in beginning actors. With practiced attention, you can easily sense and overcome it. Until you develop your "third eye," a friend or coach can help you spot such behavior.

If you feel like you've been standing still, find impulses for your character to move. Emotional reactions are a good motivator—movement expresses internal feelings. Or you could find something else in the environment to move toward, like going to the office water cooler, or looking out a window.

Beware of too much visualization, which for many people requires a lot of concentration. Instead, focus outward on your space objects, and try to be deliberate about where you place them on the stage. Visualization and placement are two topics I'll talk a lot more about in Chapter 7, when we look at building an environment for the scene.

Hand-Waving (Aka "Charlie-Brown-Ing")

Hand-waving is the classic example of bad object work, using indistinct hand motions to create miracles. I also call it "Charlie-Brown-ing," and once you see it this way, you won't be able to un-see it.

One of my favorite TV cartoons is *A Charlie Brown Christmas*, based on the *Peanuts* comic strip by Charles Schultz. It's well over fifty years old now, and the animation quality is understandably of its time. You can find clips from it online.

Near the end of this story, Charlie Brown has visited the local Christmas tree seller to decorate the set for his friends' Nativity play. He's picked an *awful* tree. It's no more than a single dried-out branch, nailed to two planks of wood, and dropping needles fast. The other kids laugh at Charlie Brown, who runs off in a fit of shame. But Linus (the wise kid) says, *"Maybe it just needs a little love."*

Together, all the kids grab a handful of lights from a nearby display and huddle around the "tree." All we see from the group is some vague waving of their hands. When they step back, what emerges is a beautifully decorated, perfectly formed, cone-shaped Christmas tree. Seconds before, the wispy little sapling couldn't support a single ornament. Now it's a Norman Rockwell beauty.

This is exactly what bad object work looks like. Inside that huddle, the kids know what they're doing to fix the tree. Whatever it is, though, it's not made clear to the audience. If we'd seen them grab a handful of pine needles and glue, it would be easier to accept that they've tripled the foliage on a dying tree branch. Instead, all we're shown is a mass of waving hands. It doesn't make sense, and the moment registers as false.[2]

Every activity—from making coffee, to opening wine bottles, to dusting shelves, to anything else—has specific steps, and each takes time. When you skip them, or rush through faster than reality would allow, all we see is a wave of your hands. Context can help us understand, but often we're left to guess. If we guess wrong, you've lost control of your scene.

Here's a simple exercise you can use to diagnose hand-waving:

Back-to-Back Activity

Two players. Give one player a real object and associated activity. It shouldn't be too complex, but should involve a few steps. Common examples include taking off one lace-up shoe and putting it back on again, or retrieving an object from a backpack. Let the other player study the object for a moment. They will perform exactly the same activity using object work.

Stand the players facing away, so they can't see each other, then both start at the same time. Do the activity at regular speed—this isn't a race. Ideally, you should see the same level of detail from both players, and they should finish at the same time. More likely, the object work player will finish first, with far less detail. Discuss the differences you observe.

It's obvious to say the solution here is to *SLOW DOWN*. But it's worth looking at why rushing happens in the first place, so we can find ways to prevent it.

---

[2] *Saturday Night Live* produced a brilliant cartoon parody of this scene. On stepping back from the perfect tree, one of the kids says, *"What did we just do?"* They go on to use their magic hand-waving power all over town, transforming objects and people into all manner of crazy things.

Thinking Ahead of the Action

Over the years, I've seen many scenes where someone is digging a hole in the ground. Gravediggers, pirates, mobsters in the woods—all these characters have a need for holes, and sometimes immediately. (*"Arrr, mateys, here come the British. Bury that treasure, quick!"*)

Have you ever dug a good-sized hole? It's hard work, and it takes some time, even in light sand or gravel. Certainly, it's going to take more than a few seconds.

And yet, when a scene calls for a character to dig, what I often see is this:

- The improviser grabs a shovel, usually out of the Void.
- They circle their arms above the floor a few times.
- *Voila!* Instant hole. The Charlie Brown kids would be proud.

What's happening here is that *the improviser is thinking too far ahead.* They have an idea to advance the scene, but for it to work, they need the hole NOW. To them, the action of digging is a roadblock. While they're creating the hole, it feels to them like nothing is happening, like the scene has stalled.[3] Rather than sit with the fear that creates, they skip the realism to get the activity done as fast as possible. They may not even be aware that they're rushing.

But realism is the *whole point* of object work. If waving your arms creates a hole in seconds, why grab the shovel at all? You might as well cast a magic spell. You have to decide—are you playing Blackbeard or Harry Potter?

Bending Reality

Another bad habit improvisers fall into to avoid "boring" activities is bending reality. You could do any number of things to make digging a hole faster or unnecessary, from simple to bizarre:

- Start digging and call a "cut to a few minutes later" (a narrative jump).
- Call in a crack team of digging experts (and hope your partners are on the ball).

---

[3] A better way to approach this might be to start the scene at the *end* of the hole-digging, but this rarely happens. I suspect it's because the improvisers are standing on a flat stage, which suggests an untouched surface. If they're thinking in levels, as I talk about later in this book, it might be easier to imagine themselves a few feet down in a freshly dug hole.

- Use a backhoe instead of a shovel.
- Endow yourself with superhero digging powers.
- Discover that the ground is cotton candy, and call in a group of toddlers to eat it.

There's nothing wrong with any of these. You set the physical laws of your world. They can be as wild as you like, and you can change them anytime. But that's also difficult, because people still need information to be able to follow what you're doing. Until you show them how your world is different, they assume your environment follows the same laws they're used to. You have to justify any and every twist. This is more work, and the resulting scene can become crazy and even more confusing.

The Solution

When improvisers unwittingly fall into these bad habits, they begin to question whether object work is worth the effort. It feels awkward and their scenes are boring, so why bother? Eventually, some players start avoiding it completely, which is everyone's loss.

Reality, however, isn't an obstacle. It's an opportunity.

A much easier way to play is to *stay present and explore the next moment*. If you fully engage with an activity, the audience will watch with interest. They may be silent, but you will have their attention. It's a good thing, even if it feels awkward. Continue to the next moment. Take your time.

What if your character *does* need a hole, fast? Knowing it takes time to dig, what's that going to do to their emotional state? What if you ramped up that tension by throwing in obstacles or activity trouble? Maybe the ground is frozen, or the shovel breaks, or the unconscious person you're trying to bury suddenly wakes up? What if time runs out?

The big benefit of thinking this way is *simplicity*. You don't need to jump ahead, creating a whole narrative about how the Pirates got the treasure, and why the British want it back, and the legend of the cursed diamond inside. You don't need to create crazy rules of gravity, or systems of Earth-controlling magic. You can make the scene all about *digging the hole*. And that scene can be just as entertaining as any other. Maybe more so, since you're not throwing in so many other random ideas.

Even the most mundane activities become exciting this way, especially for YOU. You're exploring the unknown, rather than rushing to the next "safe" idea. That's *real* improvisation.

And yes, it's also terrifying.

Good object work takes *courage*. When you're playing the reality of an activity, it can feel like nothing is happening. The fear constantly pushes you to speed up, to cut corners. Be brave. Fight that instinct. In slowing down, you will discover unique opportunities to play.

Powering through Obstacles

A single player picks any improvised activity, for example, paddling a canoe, and commits to performing it as realistically as possible. The coach calls out various problems as obstacles to the activity; for example, *"The paddle breaks!"* or *"The canoe is sinking!"* or *"You're attacked by mosquitoes!"* No matter what happens, the player must adapt to keep performing the activity. Avoid "magical" solutions to problems—stay in the moment and play the reality as much as possible. As a fully solo exercise, the player can introduce their own obstacles.

Part III

Environment

You create an improv setting from empty space and a few chairs, but it's no less significant than the intricate backdrop of a Broadway production. Improv has one big advantage: you can build and replace your sets instantly, creating anything you can imagine. You don't even need a gang of IATSE members to do the heavy lifting.

That said, there's no doubt that a visible set draws people into a story more easily than an improvised one. Our challenge in improv is to create the same sense of place.

In this part of the book, we'll explore the mechanics of creating the worlds your characters inhabit.

You Will Learn

- how to start a scene with an activity, without clichés;
- techniques for building detailed "virtual sets";

- additional tools for establishing and refreshing your environment, including some that don't rely on your mobility;
- why and how to research environmental detail to get new ideas; and
- special considerations for outdoor scenes and unusual environments.

6

Starting with Where

You're standing center stage. You've introduced yourself to the audience and maybe got a starting suggestion. The lights are about to come up. *What will you do first?*

The opening offer of any improvisation is important because it's really the only free idea. Everything afterward unfolds in reaction to the first moment. Not every scene needs a Where,[1] but we can often choose to start there. Creating a sense of place gives you and your audience a solid platform for what comes next.

Establishing a Where is nearly always done through an activity. It's a good choice because it can quickly link you to more ideas. The activity suggests the location. The location suggests characters who might be there and why. And as we've seen, playing with routines can easily give those characters a starting objective. Because activities are such fertile ground, beginning improvisers are usually taught to start scenes this way.

Soon, however, students run into a big problem. Patterns of behavior develop, and starting this way becomes repetitive and predictable. We

---

[1] As mentioned in our First Principles from Chapter 2.

typically see the first player step forward and wave their hands, waiting. A second player comes in and comments on the activity, and then the two argue over what they're doing. You may hear people refer to scenes like this as *"cutting carrots,"* from the stereotype that every awful kitchen scene seems to involve someone chopping vegetables for dinner.

Rather than explore ways to fix this problem, most training moves on to more "advanced" elements for starting scenes, through character, relationship, premise, and/or dialogue. Starting with an activity comes to be thought of as "training wheels" for the improviser, and this is one way object work gets a bad reputation.

I agree that, for variety's sake, we should start our scenes with many different types of offers. Even so, we easily forget how much inspiration we can pull from environment. To avoid clichés, we just have to explore different ways to use it as a starting point.

The Three Environments

Here again we get help from Viola Spolin. She wrote that an improv scene actually has *three environments* to keep in mind:

1. **Immediate.** This is the area within your arm's reach that you can manipulate through object work. In an office scene, for example, it's the desk you're working at.
2. **General.** This is the area in which the scene takes place —the office with other desks, file cabinets, water cooler, etc. When we specify a scene's location, we're usually defining the general environment.
3. **Larger.** This is the area beyond the scene—the office building, the traffic outside the window, the city.

We can draw ideas from any of these environments, which gives us an expanded list of places to start from.

Beginners tend to stay in the *immediate* environment. The lights come up to find someone working at their desk, and they don't move from there.[2] The

---

[2] Remember the bad habit of *rooting* from Chapter 5? If you're too internally focused, such as trying to think of something clever to do, you may not move around that much when performing the activity.

audience might guess that this is an office, but they don't see it. This is a desk in the Void.

Instead, you could start from one part of the *general* environment and then move to another. What if we find you stage right, pulling a file out of the cabinet, and then returning to work at the desk? Or grabbing a cup of water from the cooler?

It's also possible to start from the *larger* environment, making an entrance from outside the office. You could then move through the general environment—hanging up your coat, pouring a coffee—before arriving at your desk. The larger environment can inspire a mood or emotional state for the character—maybe you're angry about the morning's traffic, or you're late . . . again. (We'll talk more about What's Beyond in Chapter 8.)

Thinking about *sub-locations* of the general environment helps you avoid clichés and "obvious" setups. Suppose you've got the suggestion of "restaurant" for a location, but don't want your scene to be yet another couple at a table. What else might be in the general environment of a restaurant that could be a different setting? Maybe you're at the salad bar, or using the restroom. Maybe dinner is over and you're paying at the register. Any of these sub-locations could give you interesting character or narrative ideas, too.

Commit and Build

Speaking of clichés, the "cutting carrots problem" is rarely caused by the activity itself. Establishing a Where is as valid a first offer as any other. It only becomes an issue if you're not using it as a foundation for something else—when you're treating it as a placeholder.

Improvisers put themselves under constant pressure to make something happen. If you don't trust your ideas, or have none at all, then to start a scene you may revert to your default basic training and dive into a random activity. This *feels* like you're doing something—by cutting carrots, you're telling your partners you're in a kitchen.

Really though, *you haven't yet started the scene*. The carrots are only there to scratch your itch to make something happen. Meanwhile, you're thinking hard for a "good" idea or waiting for a partner to bail you out. With no point to the activity, you might as well stand there holding a sign saying, *"I'm in a kitchen. Come help me!*" Your first offer is meaningless and the scene is already in trouble.

One big hint that this is happening is hand-waving—you're not present with the activity, so it's muddled and repetitive. Another hint is that once the scene gets going, the cutting carrots stops and never gets picked up again.

Make that first offer count! *Commit* your full focus and engagement to the activity, then *build* on it to advance the scene. You don't have to wait for a partner. As long as you're making discoveries from the environment, an audience will watch you with interest.

Many players learn this only on those rare occasions when no one enters and they're forced to do the scene alone. Then they start advancing on their activity because they have no other choice. This is the mindset *every* improviser needs. When starting a scene, you must treat it as though you'll be the only one in it. Because until someone bravely steps in, you ARE the only one in it!

This may seem challenging, especially if you're a newer improviser. So let's look at how you commit and build.

Note and Make Choices

Building on your own activity isn't a new idea, or even a revolutionary one. In fact, it's so dead obvious that I overlooked it for years, and I meet students all the time who haven't picked up on it. We're often so focused on exploring others' ideas and offers, we forget it's also possible to explore our own.

It takes practice and experience to build your improviser's "third eye." Once you do, though, improv becomes much less stressful. You never have to start with a fully formed idea. You can take *any* random activity and discover meaning in it, simply by noting your physicality with the objects and using that to make choices.

For example, you don't have to start the scene knowing you're a chef in a fancy restaurant that's got a critic visiting later that evening. You just start cutting carrots and pay attention to how you're doing it. In a moment I'll have a warning for you about this. But here's one way you might arrive at those character, location, and narrative choices, simply by being curious about what you're doing:

1. Watching your object work, you notice you're cutting those carrots very quickly. This suggests you have some knife skills. (You can now play with that idea, chopping with flair, which provides *visual interest*.)

2. What kind of person might have knife skills? A chef. (Now you have a *character* choice. This also gives you a clue to the *location*—it's a restaurant kitchen.)

3. Why would a chef, leader of the kitchen, be doing the lowly job of cutting carrots? Maybe they want this dish to be perfect. (You might now get the idea to be more specific in how you cut the carrots—more *visual interest*. You've also decided this chef is a control freak, which is a *character point of view*.)

4. Why must this dish be so perfect? Because a critic is coming tonight. (That's *narrative*. And the chef is under unusual pressure, which gives you a *dynamic* or *emotion* to play with.)

These choices can occur in the space of a few seconds if you're open to exploring. You do this all the time when improvising with others—why not do it with yourself too?

Here's the warning: *make just ONE choice at a time*. It's easy to look at the process above and think you have to work all this out at once. You don't. All you need is *one* small inspiration that gives the activity meaning. It only takes one to push the scene in a new direction. This thought experiment simply illustrates that you can make these *types* of choices instinctively by paying attention to the details of the routine.

The main point is, in the critical opening seconds of a scene, you're not waiting for someone else to bring an idea. You're making a strong opening offer by committing to the activity and building on it.

Noting and making choices also allows for infinite variations. On a different night, you might notice something different about the carrots. The resulting choice and those that follow will lead you to different scenes.

Now, even if you're able to come up with a complex scene premise this way, it's important to hold these ideas loosely. As long as you're alone at the start of a scene, you're in control. When a partner joins you, it's tempting to steamroll them. (*"You are late! The restaurant critic will be here any minute! Pick up that knife and help me with the salad!"*) Instead, let your partner provide their own offer, and be ready for them to take things in a different direction. Keep your choices ready to use or throw away as the scene progresses.

Noting Your Physicality

Single player starts with a space object. They handle the object and let it help them make strong decisions about character and location. Expand the activities to further define Who they are and Where.

Do this exercise slowly at first. The coach can prompt if the player seems stuck. Some example prompts: *"Are you doing it fast or slow?"* *"Is it important to you?"* *"Do you like this activity?"* Continue to prompt *"What does that suggest?"*

Remember Your Eye Contact!

Watching your own activity means observing it with your improviser's eye. It doesn't mean staring at your hands. Keep your head up and make eye contact with your partner!

It's easy to get very focused on objects and forget to do this, which kills any connection you have with your fellow players. That's why you must practice object work away from the stage, so you can do it without looking down.

What if the activity needs the *character* to be very focused, like wristwatch repair or bomb disposal? Eye contact still applies! When your partner speaks, be affected—let it draw you up from the activity so you're talking face to face. Then turn back to what you're working on. You can also use your peripheral vision to keep an eye on what's going on around you.

Be ready to *drop the activity* if you find it's pulling too much of your focus. It's better to stay connected to your partner than lose track of the scene.

Focused Work

A single player chooses and performs an activity with small objects and very fine detail, for example, needlepoint, painting tiny figurines, building a model airplane. Maintain this activity while carrying on a conversation, with the coach or another player working separately.

Coaches: Watch for repetition or loss of detail, which are hints the player is losing focus.

Conversation with Involvement

Two or three players. They agree on a simple topic of discussion and keep it going while they eat and drink a large meal. Keep the focus on eating and talking so this doesn't become a "scene" that avoids the exercise. Show the objects on the table. Chew and swallow your food!

Try this also with a larger group as a dinner party. Players can decide who they are as a group and individually. Everyone should stay engaged in a conversation, even if there is more than one around the table.

Focus on How Instead of Why

Why your character is doing an activity is an introspective question. Reasons are often complex and can get you stuck in your head. Asking *How* is more observational. It forces you to see the detail in what you're doing, which helps you make connections. Your ideas will tend to be more character- and emotion-based, which are more flexible. Focusing on *How* first can actually help the *Why* come easier.

Exploring Activity Movements

A solo player chooses an activity. As they perform it, choose any single movement that reoccurs as part of the activity. Keeping the overall activity, the player then explores changing up that movement, for example, making it faster/slower, harder/gentler, bigger/smaller. The coach can provide direction if necessary.

Notice how changes to the movement can suggest changes to character.

Change Your Attitude

I'm 100 percent confident about this commit-and-build process. In the many years I've used it, noting my own activity and making choices about it has never failed to give me at least an idea. They're not always great, but ideas always appear.

However, if you're anxious about being stumped, there's a fallback you can use. Ask yourself, *"What's my attitude here?"* No matter what's going on, even if it's nothing, you can *always* have an opinion about what you're doing. Strong characters have a point of view, and exploring attitude will naturally change up the way you're performing the activity. This will give you something to notice and make choices about.

Oakville Improv's Duncan McKenzie made a great observation to me: most beginners choose to perform activities with bored resentment. A better default choice is *excited enthusiasm*.[3]

Exploring Activity Attitudes

A solo player chooses an activity. The player continues to perform the activity as the coach calls out various attitudes they must take on. (Try some of these: satisfied, proud, excited, enthusiastic, confident, uncomfortable, bored, resentful, guilty, suspicious, secretive, anxious, disgusted, or any others you can think of.) Try to balance positive and negative attitudes.

Notice how changes to the attitude can completely change the activity. You can explore that point of view for even more ideas within scenes.

---

[3] Many players also get stuck in the belief that comedy is always about people being terrible at something. It can be just as funny to watch them be super-successful.

7

Building Worlds

With a process for creating strong starting offers, we now move on to the physical techniques you use to show the environment. There are two big questions. How do you decide what to show? And where do you put everything?

These questions can be intimidating for the beginning improviser. Let's try to make this as simple as possible so we can still focus on character, relationship, and all the other elements of a scene. But remember, *Tools Not Rules!* The approach I describe in this chapter will help you practice, but it shouldn't become a fixed method.

Stage Picture

The first thing we can control is the *stage picture*—what the audience is physically able to see. Through the placement of furniture and people on the stage, we create visual interest. If the players huddle together in one corner, we get the sense of a tight, claustrophobic space. Spreading everything across the stage tells us we're in an open expanse. By changing up the stage picture from time to time, you're working in a much richer world. This can be especially helpful for long-form, where lengthy scenes in a blank space can cause visual fatigue.

When starting a scene, think first about your chairs. For safety and to avoid distraction, clear furniture and physical props from previous scenes. Then set the chairs you need to support your idea. If you want a living room couch, for example, you can put two to three chairs together. Setting more than one chair can also be a signal you want a partner to join you.

Then, make a choice about where on the stage to start. Front and center is the usual place, but you can create a mood by starting somewhere else. What does it suggest to start in an upstage corner, or right on the apron?

As the scene begins, other players can find ways to help fill in the stage picture. In your basic restaurant scene, for example, two people start at a table, scanning the menu. But how many restaurants in the world have a *single table*? Players can add other tables of diners nearby, creating the sense of a busy restaurant. These people aren't involved characters, they're part of the background, like extras in a movie. Yet they can still affect the tone of the scene. What happens to the stakes of a breakup conversation when we can see other couples within earshot?

In fact, most public places have people passing through. Office employees can walk past a conversation between a boss and assistant, dog walkers can stroll through a park. Every improvisation is full of opportunities to add to the stage picture. Players can also portray objects and props in the scene — more about this in Chapter 10.

In playing with stage picture, be especially careful of your expectation around entrances. Not everyone who comes on stage has to be a point of focus. As a player already in the scene, the temptation is to immediately address anyone who comes in, to involve them in the action. Instead, just continue your scene and allow new players to establish themselves. It should be very obvious when they're joining as new characters or filling in the stage picture. You can always choose to bring a character out of the stage picture and into focus, but you don't have to.

When entering for stage picture, do it simply and quickly. Try to be as unobtrusive as possible. Avoiding exaggeration signals the current players that you're filling in the background.

Stage Picture (Background)

Two or three players in a location where other people are commonly present. As they play a scene, other players should step in to occupy the background, filling in the stage picture. They can be stationary or passing through. Background players should be "alive" but not distracting.

The Problem with Visualization

With stage picture in mind, let's now add improvised activity and objects. We've talked about the importance of clarity and specificity in object work. Because of this, you may think you need a clear and specific picture of the place *in mind* before you can create it for the audience.

You don't. That may seem contradictory, but let me explain.

At some point in your improv training, you've likely read or heard instructions to *"see the space."* Ideally, visualization helps you experience a scene's environment by mapping your mind's eye image onto the stage. For example, by picturing yourself standing in a stage-sized kitchen, you can walk around inside that picture, interacting with the sink, refrigerator, and other appliances you "see."

Many improv instructors use extended visualization exercises, leading students through dreamlike landscapes or rooms filled with dozens of objects.[1] These can be useful for training focus and intuition, letting go of manufactured ideas and contacting direct experience. Many people (including myself) find these exercises delightful and transformative.

The problem is, these visualizations are solo explorations, unattached to performance. For me at least, holding an image in mind *while improvising a scene* is much more challenging. Visualization uses a lot of brain power, which makes it harder to work with all the other things you have to keep track of.

Moving around inside a visualized location is also problematic when you have to consider the audience's viewpoint. Maybe your imagined sink is on

---

[1] There are several examples in Mary Scruggs and Michael Gellman's book *Process: An Improviser's Journey*.

the opposite side of the kitchen from the fridge, but you don't want to turn away from the audience to use it. So you end up shifting things around in your image to fit the stage, which is even more difficult.

Many improvisers have admitted to me that they've *never* been able to visualize.[2] It's a big reason why they've given up trying to be more physical. If that's you, take heart: my position is that "seeing the space" is absolutely unnecessary.

Placement

It's natural to want to create a complete picture for the audience. Unfortunately, that's out of your hands. As you reveal details, one at a time, each person watching will build their own picture. That's fine, though; you *want* the audience to visualize the scene. To help them, all you have to do is be deliberate about the details you show and where you place them on the stage.

I'm not anti-visualization. Mentally picturing objects and places can help you recall details that might not otherwise come to mind. But rather than insist on it, the technique of *placement* is a more practical approach. When your kitchen scene needs a refrigerator, make a choice of where to place it, then show us some detail—which way the door opens, something inside, and so on. Whether you actually see a refrigerator in your head isn't necessary. You're marking a specific location on the stage with the *idea* of a fridge. Done skillfully, the audience accepts that idea and adds it to their mental picture. They see the kitchen while you get on with the story.

Once you've placed the refrigerator, though, everyone must remain aware that that part of the stage is now occupied, just as if a fridge was really there. It's also essential that every player handles the object the same exact way, in the same exact place. We call this *object permanence*, and if you violate it, you break the audience's visualization. They notice. If it's a small detail out of place, like a shelf at a slightly different height, they can adjust. If it's something big, like opening the door in the opposite direction, or walking through the occupied space, their picture collapses. They see you improvising, and they're not caught up in the story anymore.

---

[2] For a few, it may be impossible. Neurologists have described a condition called "aphantasia," where a person is completely unable to visualize or recall any other sensory experience beyond the present moment. It's estimated that up to 2 percent of all people have this condition, and there may be a spectrum of ability as well. https://aphantasia.com/what-is-aphantasia/

Don't underestimate how powerful this is! You can actually see the reaction ripple through an audience. It's like they've been startled awake from a dream. They shift in their seats, sometimes they even murmur to themselves. It's equally powerful when all players respect object permanence. I've heard screams of laughter when improvisers remember to sidestep a table or trip over the same loose rug.

Generally, you'll want to place objects so everyone can see you working with them. For example, placing the refrigerator on the front of the stage lets you face the audience as you look inside. Beyond that, your virtual set doesn't have to conform to a logical floor plan.

To make remembering placements easier, look for reference markers that can help you return to the same place, like spots on the floor, or how things line up with seats in the audience. Don't worry about this too much—you can get away with being a few inches off.

Above all, focus on *one object at a time* as you need them. Trying to paint a whole scene creates too many things for you to remember. Create objects as required for activities or events in the scene.

To sum up: place objects deliberately, remember where they are, and treat them consistently. These are the steps for creating environments the audience can see, without taking too much brain power from the rest of your improv.

Hopefully, you now see why everything we talked about in Part II: Object Work (Chapters 3–5) is such a big deal. Because you're not alone—*everyone in your scene is doing the same thing.* You need great skills to be able to communicate, remember, and build on each other's placements and activities. That's how improvisers create rich, believable worlds together.

Object permanence demands a good visual-spatial working memory to track and remember everyone's placements. That may not come easily to some players, which is why it's important to regularly practice your Where exercises. Here are two excellent ones:

The Where Game

Player 1 decides on a location and shows Where through an object or activity. When an outside player thinks they know Where, they can assume a character and enter the location. Players establish relationships with the location and each other through objects. Keep the focus on the environment—character is secondary in this exercise.

Fix a Problem, Leave a Problem

Decide on a location in advance. Each player passes through, one by one, contacting all objects established. Each player discovers one problem in the environment that they fix, for example, water puddle on the floor, broken doorknob. They also create one different problem and leave it behind. Players don't have to establish new objects but will probably have to. There can be more than one problem at a time, but keeping track of too many problems will make things difficult. Watch for consistency of objects: doors opening the same way, and so on.

Pre-Fab Sets

Can we make this even simpler? Here's a radical idea: *why not build your improvised sets in advance?* Many locations pop up again and again in improv: living rooms, kitchens, offices. If you already have a set layout in mind, you can instantly inhabit these places rather than take time and energy to figure out what's there.

Try this with your improv team. In your notebook, make a list of common locations. Then draw small scene diagrams for each, as if you were designing the set for a stage play. What objects are there, and where are they? Lay it all out on the diagram. Be as detailed as you like.

Next, take a diagram onto your stage and give your fellow players a tour of the room. Point out all the details and their locations. Practice interacting with the objects so everyone treats them consistently. The result is a set you can now use for future scenes. When you use it, you'll feel more confident knowing where you are.

You can also agree on an accompanying stage picture. Where will you put the physical chairs, if any? Are there certain types of people who tend to be present? Any player not in the scene then knows what they can do to fill in the background.

Using a *"pre-fab"* set like this isn't cheating. You're just starting with a known location you can still use spontaneously. In your office scenes, from lights up you'll know there's a desk to your left, with a computer and a wonky mouse. You know there's a bookshelf in the corner beside a little tea table.

Whether any of these objects come into use is still flexible. YOU know they're all there, and you can use them however you like.

This has big benefits for players who regularly perform together. You can quickly call out a set—*"And now we take you to this bachelor apartment . . ."*—and the whole team knows where they are. When everyone knows the placements in advance, there's less negotiation of physical offers and fewer dangers of blocking.

If you don't play with a regular group, you can still design sets for your own use. But remember that the objects in your set aren't established reality until you place them for that scene. Keep your eyes open. If another player puts a file cabinet downstage left, and your pre-fab set usually has it upstage right, you still have to recognize the one downstage. Maybe there are two cabinets in this scene, or maybe you have to leave yours out. Be flexible and work with your partners.

The easiest pre-fab sets to use are locations from your own life. You already know where everything is in your bedroom, kitchen, etc. It doesn't mean you're playing the scene in *YOUR* kitchen. It's just a place that happens to have the same layout.

Location Tour

As "homework," players study a room in their home, office, or other familiar place. They commit to memory as much detail about the furniture and objects as they can. In class, they give a tour of the room as it would fit on the stage, placing objects and describing the layout. After the tour, other players can join to perform a scene in that location.

[Variation] During the tour, player adds stories (real or fictional) about why some items are there. This provides additional background which may be useful in the following scene.

Where with Set Pieces

Create a list of props and furniture. Teams of players create different scenes using the same list of objects. Experiment with agreeing where the props are in advance, or starting with just the list in mind. Try to let the Where create the scene, rather than impose a scene on the objects.

Technical Assistance

You can also get help from offstage to create the environment. If you're lucky to have a theatre where you're in control of lights and sound, add a *technical improviser* to your shows. Experiment with different types of lighting effects. Spotlights, shapes, washes, and gobos create specific looks and inspire the players on the stage. Build a library of sound effects and music clips to add to your sound board—there are plenty of computer apps to help you organize these and get to them quickly when you have an idea.

Remember the technical improviser gives and takes just like any other player. They can use lighting or sound changes as offers in the middle of a scene, not just as setups.

And of course, your *music director* can always add mood music or sound effects too.

Another Thought Experiment

To put all this together, let's explore how I might set up a scene with environment and then return to it later for more ideas.

Suppose I ask the audience for a location, and I get "a church." Specificity always helps details spring to mind, so a good first choice to make is, what kind of church? Is it the Vatican cathedral? Is it a country chapel? Is it my neighborhood church? The decision influences what details I might discover. I remember a trip I took to Italy a few years ago, so the Vatican inspires me.

Now, the Vatican is still a big place that feels very abstract, so it probably helps to have a sub-location. It could be the altar, a pew, a confessional booth, a table serving tea and sandwiches, a priest's office, the catacombs—anything that comes to mind when I think of a church in general, or the Vatican specifically.

As always, pick just one idea. The first thing that comes to mind for me is the altar, so that's where I'll start the scene. This thought process is how you take a vague, boring suggestion like "a church" and make it interesting.

Now, to build my environment. Stage picture first. I decide I don't need any chairs or props right now. If it turns out I have to sit down later, I can always grab one.

Next, I decide to place the altar down front. What's a detail I can use to show it to the audience? I recall that the Vatican altar was made of marble, so

I start with a polishing activity, which lets me show its surface and size. Here's where I commit to my activity and start building on it.

Noting my physicality suggests to me I'm a janitor—a priest wouldn't be doing this kind of work. Then I notice I'm a bit sloppy with it. Maybe I'm not enjoying my work—a janitor who's not feeling very religious?

It's very hard to describe this on the page without it seeming like a lot of breakdown, a lot of *thinking*. But after much practice with physical improv, these choices happen instinctively for me, within the space of a few seconds. You do this in your scenes, too—one idea free-associating to the next. From the starting suggestion of "a church," then making discoveries from my physicality, now I'm a Vatican janitor having a crisis of faith. Behold the power of environment work—*hallelujah!*

As I continue the scene, I can always turn back to the environment and discover more ideas. To get some guidance for my existential angst, I decide to visit the confessional. So I place the booth, keeping in mind where I placed the altar so I don't pass through it and confuse everyone. I decide the booth is stage left, open a door, and step inside.

What could I discover in here? I could crouch onto a kneeler. Or pick up a Bible. There's a panel between me and where the priest sits that slides open and closed. These are all things I can play with, by discovering one more detail at a time as I need them. And as the janitor, I could continually be cleaning everything, behavior I could explore throughout the scene.

Do I have to actually see any of this in my mind's eye? NO! When I discover something, I simply place it through object work, then maintain the reality of that object where I placed it. If I do a good job, the audience fills in other details on their own. They're the ones who see the cathedral. I don't have to.

If my fellow players love to do scenes in churches, this cathedral might even become a pre-fab set for us to use in the future. Our technical improviser can also join in, playing a bell-ringing sound or adjusting the lights for a suitable church mood.

And this is still just the first few moments of the scene. Imagine what happens when the Pope enters to take my confession!

Now, go back and do a thought experiment of your own, based on "a church." Free-associate your own ideas, then think through how you might set up your scene, one idea at a time. Take as much time as you need—it's all in your head, so the pressure is off! As I said before, mental rehearsals train your mind and your instincts so that you do *less* thinking in performance. Combine this with regular scene practice and you'll learn to make strong physical choices very quickly.

8

Refreshing the Environment

As you get drawn into the events of an improvisation, there's a tendency for the environment to fade away. You may become aware you've been standing still for a long time, or that your previous scenes have all been slow and talky.

Returning to the Where keeps things fresh, for you and the audience. If you're getting stuck in your head, it grounds you in the scene and helps you focus outward. You can use the techniques in this chapter anytime you want to refresh your environment or discover new things. They also include ways for players to help from outside the scene.

Big Energy and Small Energy

When we want to add physical energy to a show, we often launch into something big—climbing a tree, or flying through the air, or some other highly active movement. These actions usually become a focal point of the scene, at least for as long as we can sustain them. *Big energy* scenes are very entertaining, and much of this book is dedicated to helping you do more of them.

Even so, you can also add energy through small details and reactions to environment that may not have anything to do with the scene.

Try this: observe the room you're in right now. What's the temperature? Are you too warm or cold? What would you do to fix that? If you're cold, you might pull a sweater off the back of your chair and put it on. You might adjust the thermostat. Maybe you just sit there and shiver.

All these actions are incidental to what you're really doing in that room, whether it's reading a book, talking with a friend, or making dinner. In improv, it's easy to overlook something like putting on a sweater because it's not related to the scene's core action. But *small energy* adds mood and nuance to a scene. It's highly effective at capturing the audience.

There are various theories as to why this happens. I think the strongest is *identification*. When you add a natural-looking small action, like drinking an improvised coffee, something in the viewer's subconscious says, *"Hey, I drink coffee, too. Somehow, we're alike!"* They begin to pay slightly more attention, moving closer to you.

Even simply crossing the stage is a small energy move. It often expresses subtext or a character's mood shift. Scripted theatre uses movement like this to break up talky scenes—you can do the same anytime.

With small energy, you don't have to be an acrobat or jump around like a crazy person. Anyone with any level of mobility can do it, even disabled performers who can't move much at all. The key is to become aware of the little things we do every day in reaction to the world around us.

To be clear, you can go too far with this, to the point where small energy becomes needless fidgeting. As always, less is more, and with experience you'll find the right balance.

Dialogue

A common "rule" taught to improvisers is *show don't tell*, meaning you shouldn't talk about what you're doing or how you're feeling when you can reveal it through action. It's a valid point, because we learn about characters through their behavior—what they say may not always be reliable. By now, though, you know how I feel about absolute rules. Used sparingly, you *can* establish environment through dialogue.

First, let's acknowledge that narrating or commenting on an activity is generally boring. (*"So, mopping the floor, eh?"* or *"You're shaving that yak wrong, you know."*) When you start talking about the object, the improvisation loses energy.

You *can* refer to environment as long as you're adding new information. Nobody says, *"Boy, it sure feels good to be chopping wood right now,"* or *"What a great holiday we're having here in Spain."* This dialogue is stilted because the characters already know these things. Instead, try to be more specific, such as, *"Boy, I need to sharpen this ax,"* or *"How about we take a side trip to Madrid tomorrow?"* These lines sound more authentic because they introduce new points for discussion.

Dialogue around objects can also set a mood. I once saw an excellent scene that opened like this: Two characters huddled together closely, shivering. One said, *"Pass me another blanket."* After a pause, the other said, *"The fire's dying."* Just two lines of dialogue and instantly there was a sense of place. However, it's important to note the scene was about two people confronting freezing to death, not arguing over survival activities.

What's Beyond?

We often define our experience through locations. Even in the boundless outdoors, we still create conceptual spaces: this parking lot, this campsite, this country. Wherever we are, though, there's always a place *beyond* which can affect us. Bringing what's beyond into the scene can help you set a mood or influence character behavior. Think of looking out the window at an approaching storm, or trying to sleep when there's a noisy party in the next room.

This is essential thinking for anyone entering an improv scene. Unless you're playing some supernatural presence that suddenly reveals itself, every entrance is a transition from the *larger* environment beyond to the *general* environment of the scene. Keeping this in mind helps you enter with much more depth.

A common problem with character entrances is the walk-on gag. It's especially popular in short-form improv. A player outside the scene spots a counterpoint to the action and rushes in with a clever joke. Once they've dropped their one-liner, though, they have nothing more to do. They lamely drift out again, or worse, they stick around and intrude into the existing character relationship, killing the momentum.[1]

---

[1] Gags do this because they're often emotionally flat. It sometimes works better when the other players have a strong reaction to the entrance.

An easy way to prevent this problem is to make a choice about *where you're coming from*. Are you returning from the bathroom? From a busy meeting in the next office? From the house next door? Inhabit that choice and you will instinctively make other choices about who you are and why you've come in here. You can still do your walk-on gag, but you also have a purpose for being there, which makes you less likely to stick out like a sore thumb afterward.[2]

Sometimes you enter by knocking on a door and waiting to be let in. Don't stand there like a zombie. (Unless you *are* a zombie, but even then you can show us something.) What's the weather like? What time of day is it? Are you carrying anything? Inhabiting the environment on your side of the door communicates information to your scene partners before you even come in. They're better able to anticipate your offer and accept your idea.

The same thinking applies to exits. You may be leaving this place, but you're entering another. Where are you going, and why? Do you need to prepare, either physically or emotionally? Make a proper exit rather than just fading into the backline.

What's Beyond?

A single player moves across the stage making an entrance and exit. They must show what location they have left and where they are going to. Think of the stage as a bare hallway you're using for the transition. No extra action takes place here other than to show what's beyond the entrance and exit.

Scene-Painting

This is a great way to drop environment onto a scene that everyone understands and can use immediately. With scene-painting, a player outside the scene steps forward and quickly narrates an object or event. Use it to add detail (*"Sally notices the green shag carpeting on the floor"*), throw a curveball into the scene (*"Suddenly the door slams shut"*), or as

---

[2] It also gives everyone a better reason to have a strong reaction to you, as in Footnote 1.

part of a transition from one beat to the next (*"Meanwhile, in an oak-paneled boardroom two floors up . . ."*). It's excellent for adding energy and visual interest to monoscenes or other long-form formats where the location tends to be static.

In short-form, when you're setting up, you have the opportunity to describe two or three things before the scene starts. This is similar to creating a pre-fab set, as we discussed in Chapter 7. For example, I might say to the audience: *"Thanks for your suggestion of an office. Let's say there's a photocopier in that corner, a desk down front right here, and on the desk is a photograph of a young woman, with cracked glass in the frame. We now take you there . . ."* I like the last object to be something specific and intriguing that gets the audience (and myself) curious. It could become important in the scene, but doesn't have to.

Just make sure your scene partners are paying attention! If you take time to describe the place, you're making a promise to the audience. If the players don't stick to your description, it will cause confusion.

Scene-Painting Intros

Practice setting up scenes by describing a few things about the location to the audience. Then play the scene, making use of the described objects.

Scene-Painting Curveballs

Have players start a scene. At one or more random points, have someone outside the scene describe something in the environment; for example, *"There's a beautiful portrait of her mother on the wall,"* or *"A large window looks out over the city skyline."* Be careful about abrupt changes which draw focus and alter the scene; for example, *"A rock crashes through the window."* Let the people in the scene work with the new information, rather than push a new direction on them.

9

Research

Most stories take place in everyday environments, but that doesn't mean they're always about everyday events. Storytelling constantly explores the unusual, and we need to vary our creative choices to keep things fresh.

As improvisers, we're trained to follow our instincts, to go with our first ideas. The problem is, our brains find comfort in safe, stable patterns of thinking. Boring scenes happen because our minds produce the same predictable, cliché, first ideas. This is especially true for environment work. How many bedroom scenes have you seen where the only object of note was the bed? It's the only thing players call to mind quickly. There are so many other things in a bedroom that could provide ideas: a book on the nightstand, a chest of drawers, a walk-in closet, a wonky ceiling fan that needs fixing.

The challenge is to train your mind to be flexible, so that less-obvious options have a chance to come to you more easily. The best way to do this is to become an active observer of your life experience. When you start taking deliberate notice of people, places, and events, it becomes easier to recall specific and unusual details when improvising.

This chapter presents some ideas for doing this research and using it in your improv. Taking the time will help you create richer environments and give you more unique ideas.

Look Around

It's very easy to lose awareness of the large number of objects around you at all times. Your brain tends to filter out a lot of detail, especially in places you're familiar with. It also chunks things together. What you think of as "a chair" might also have a pillow on it or a blanket draped over the back.

Look around the room you're in right now. Chances are pretty good you'll see more individual objects than you can easily count. You might even notice a few things you've forgotten were there.

Once you start observing, you'll notice that *every* environment is like this, even places we think of as "empty." For example, I often teach workshops in a multipurpose room at a community center. When I enter that room, my first impression is always that it's barren. Looking closer, I see chairs stacked in the corner, a table, a clock, a fire extinguisher, a sign with building policies printed on it, and more.

Environments also have features we don't think of as objects, but which influence our experience of that place. Rooms have doors and windows. There might be carpet, hardwood flooring, or industrial tile. What kind of lighting is there? Where's the nearest electrical outlet to where you're sitting?

Notice also that most things you see in an environment are "typical" to that place. That's why they're there instead of somewhere else. If you spot something that's out of place, why is it there? Is there a story behind it? This can give you the beginning of a narrative idea.

Think back to my Vatican example in Chapter 7. Of course I could still do that scene without having visited the cathedral. But when I was there, taking deliberate note of details helped me later on when coming up with ideas for my improvised Vatican.

Remember, it's not your job to visualize or reproduce all this detail when you improvise. You're simply noting the contents of the real-world environment so that it's easier for those ideas to come back to you later.

Once you've done this "homework" for a while, the following exercises can help practice your recall.

Finding Objects in the Immediate Environment

Three or more players agree on a simple group relationship and a topic of discussion. While the discussion proceeds, each player must handle objects found in the environment. Try not to invent objects, but rather discover them. Keep the discussion going! There should be dozens of objects by the end.

Create an Object, Say a Line

Two or three players. Like the previous exercise, but players can choose any location, character, and activity. They can speak a next line of dialogue only after they have established a new object in the environment. It must be a new object, not a new activity or new use for the same object.

Sound Effects

Sound is easy to communicate and has powerful effects. Listen to the sounds that objects and activities make and think about how you might reproduce them.

A technical improviser with a stocked sound board is a great help. Much of the time, though, you'll use your voice to create effects. You've probably seen beat-boxers and stand-up comics with incredible talent,[1] but don't think you have to operate at their level—approximations of sound are fine. For what they give you, it's worth the effort to try.

A good example is entering a scene by knocking on a door. When miming the knock, many improvisers tap their foot to create the sound. That's a good instinct, but it makes you look like a trick pony doing math calculations. It's also limiting — by vocalizing different sounds, you can be hesitantly tapping or angrily pounding. The sound effect makes a strong character offer before you even enter the room.

Two notes on using sound effects in performance. First, don't cop out by using real words ("*Knock, knock, knock!*"). This comes off as a goofy comment on the improv and spoils your illusion. It can also be confusing—depending

---

[1] One of the best is Michael Winslow. If you're of a certain age, you might remember him from the *Police Academy* movies. You can find clips of his act online, but avoid the movies—they have NOT held up well.

on the situation or the words you use, players or audience may think your character is actually speaking dialogue.

Second, don't overuse sound effects unless you're deliberately playing a game with them. Too many tend to pull focus from other elements of a scene.

Use All Five Senses

As I write this, I'm visiting a friend's house in Nova Scotia, looking out over the coastline. It's a gorgeous summer afternoon. The sunlight is dancing on the rippling surface of the ocean. A gentle breeze cools my skin and fills my nose with a fresh, salty odor. Hummingbirds chirp at each other. Somewhere out of sight, a motorboat drones across the bay. My lips are still salty from a swim earlier. (This is a pretty sweet place to get some work done.)

How much richer is that description than *"I'm on the back deck near the water?"* In entertainment especially, we spend so much time looking and listening. We forget the power of our other senses to create experience. When you're observing sights and sounds, also open yourself to what you can smell, taste, and feel in the environment.

These sensations are hard to communicate to an audience, but your awareness of them inspires actions and character choices. If you feel a draft, it might send you looking for a sweater.[2] If there's a salty taste, maybe you decide your character works as a french fry vendor.

In the rush to make scenes happen, we often forget our characters *live* in the environments we create. Take a moment to experience their world. Inhale the sea air and sigh. Speak louder to be heard over the pounding surf. Be disgusted by the over-salted french fries. When you feel these moments, the audience feels them too.

Movie Magic

We love movies and TV because they're so immersive—they draw us into their worlds. Creating improv with the feel of a big-budget movie has been an ambitious goal throughout my career.

---

[2] Temperature (too warm or cold) is often a strong motivator for characters. As I get older, I feel cold *ALL THE TIME*, and it turns me into a grumpy old man.

The amount of work that filmmakers put into crafting a realistic setting is astounding. Production teams spend weeks building sets and creating effects, often for shots that last only seconds.

Although your improv illusion powers are more limited (not to mention your production budget), you can use similar techniques to create immersive scenes.

Try this: go to YouTube and find a scene from a favorite movie—genre doesn't matter. Look for a wide-angle shot of the set, then pause the video and study the background. What are the "typical" objects in that place? Does anything stand out? If it's an artificial set, what have the designers put there to make it look real? Note that even scenes shot on location are often deliberately decorated.

Now run the scene through and notice how the film communicates other senses. What would it feel like to actually be in that place? What's the temperature—do the characters seem to be chilled or sweating? What noises are in the background?

Are special visual effects used? How do they look? Could you re-create them on stage, maybe with the help of sound?

Look at how the director uses the camera to create mood or communicate information. What's the effect of a wide shot vs. a close-up? Are there unusual perspectives or editing tricks? How are the cuts between shots paced to match the energy of the scene?

You can also research film and TV from specific genres to learn the common elements of film noir, westerns, sci-fi, and so on. If you know in advance you'll be doing an improvisation based on a specific film or TV show, it makes sense for players to research it together and discuss what you could use. You might agree on a pre-fab set and other well-known details, like sound effects or lighting.

Film is a gold mine for your improv. In Chapter 13, I'll show you some easy techniques for creating cinematic flair, including camera angles, split-screens, and so on. They're fun to play with and audiences love them.

Location Tour with Movie Scenes

Students study a clip from their favorite film or TV show. Commit to memory as much detail about the scene as possible, as discussed above. In class, describe the environment as an improvised set. After describing, add other students to perform a scene in that location. If special effects or camera tricks are used, can you replicate them?

10

Unusual Environments

An improvisation can go anywhere, anytime. When your scene happens in an unusual environment, you may find it momentarily disorienting. It's easy to get lost in the idea, trying to visualize the place and communicate its strangeness.

But whether you're in a local coffee shop or a medieval swamp castle on Mars, the techniques for establishing environment are exactly the same. Find a single object or activity and start there. It can also help to decide whether your *character* finds the place unusual. If they live there, it's normal and familiar to them, which may give you a way into the idea. Attitude and scene context can often convey the fantasy of a place to the audience, with little extra effort on your part.[1]

Here are some more thoughts on unusual places and strange activities.

The Great Outdoors

A lot of people spend most of their time indoors. They forget about the world outside until they have need for errands, exercise, or transportation

---

[1] In Chapter 12, I'll give you an easy technique that can also help with unusual suggestions.

to yet another indoor space. This isn't great for variety in improv. Indoor environments are nearly always the same—square rooms with furniture—which gives a similar feel to every scene.

Remember Viola Spolin's concept of the three environments: immediate, general, and larger? When you're indoors, the larger environment is often forgotten, obscured behind the walls. In the outdoors, it's right there with you, inescapable. There's a wider range of conditions and objects to interact with. And nature is always changing.

People are much more affected by environment when outside. It brings all your senses into awareness. The air carries different smells, more and stranger sounds. Temperature and lighting can change quickly. The whole world feels different when you don't have a ceiling over your head.

When playing outdoor scenes, I recommend you always make a choice about the *time of day*. The same place will feel much different depending on whether it's light or dark.[2] You should also consider the *weather*, even to decide it's a pleasant day. These starting conditions will affect other choices.

Since you're performing in an indoor theatre, it can be tough to avoid indoor thinking. (Lucky you if you get to play outside!) Remember that the outdoors extend in all directions, including up, and sometimes down. Expand your awareness to the larger environment beyond the stage. You can notice distractions (like bats flying by) or events that may soon impact you (like that volcano erupting).

One thing to be careful of is talking about what you see. Since you can't easily interact with things in the distance, sometimes you will need to break the "rule" of *show don't tell*. Try not to overdo it, though. If you can, bring the event toward you as soon as possible, so you can use your physical skills. A storm on the horizon should be raining on you before too long. That bird in the sky might poop on you, which sends you looking for your rifle for revenge. Find a physical choice whenever you can.

Outdoor locations are also great for introducing a different type of conflict—you versus nature. If your team finds your characters are arguing all the time, put them into a hostile outdoor environment. Maybe they'll work together to survive.

---

[2] Come to think of it, time of day is a good choice for *any* scene, since the character choices for day-timers and night-owls can be very different.

> ## Exploration of a Larger Environment/ Weather Exercise
>
> Players choose an outdoor location and agree on characters and activity. They then explore the environment. Players should be affected by conditions beyond the immediate space. What is above? What is below? Be affected by weather and outdoor conditions. Try to show as much as you can without using dialogue.

Playing Animals and Objects

One of my driving principles is to *help people see the object whenever possible.* When an improvised object becomes especially significant to a scene, or if it's something particularly unusual, it begs to be physically played by another improviser.

This happens a lot with animals. Someone will introduce a dog/cat/horse/cow and do a great job showing it to us as a space object. They'll pet it, watch it move around, or let it jump up on them, whatever. But an animal is a living thing, and it's difficult to keep that going. If you're on the outside, jump in and show us the creature! This rarely fails to energize a scene and wake up an audience.

If you're coming in as an animal, you don't have to come in on all fours. Try communicating its physicality in different ways. For example, gorillas lead with their heads when they move, so you can lean forward and swing your arms. Some animals (especially reptiles and insects) stand very still for long periods of time, and then scurry quickly to a different place. Spend an afternoon watching a few nature videos—you'll pick up some great ideas.

You can achieve similar effects by playing props and furniture. I once saw a sketch condensing *Raiders of the Lost Ark* into a two-minute trailer. The actors created all the objects using their bodies. One tumbled across the stage as the giant boulder that nearly crushes Indiana Jones. Others used their arms to recreate the pit of snakes. They floated around as the wispy spirits that melt the bad guys' faces off at the end. It was a real crowd-pleaser—obviously rehearsed, but it's just as easy to do similar things in improv, even for more mundane props.

Use this sparingly. Adding more than one prop or animal can be a fantastic game, but when many improvisers join in quickly it usually derails the scene. Also note that these are *environmental offers,* NOT characters. Your intention should be to add to the stage picture. If other players involve you as a character, then have at it. Otherwise, it's very easy to pull focus and become a distraction, especially with animals. To protect the scene, you may have to consider exiting just as quickly as you entered.

Be careful with your body! Choices like these will stretch your physicality, and it's easy to injure yourself. Be especially mindful when using other players as furniture—you could hurt them physically or emotionally. For more tips, please visit Part V on Safety.

Human Props

Two or three players start a scene with any information they want. Throughout, they discover objects or creatures in the scene. Other players join to become those objects, which the characters handle (safely). Outside players can also jump in as objects and allow the characters in the scene to discover what they are.

Animal Characters

Practice as a group. Everyone chooses an animal, and moves about the space as that animal. The animals don't interact. Take time to play with the physical movements of the animal.

This exercise can also help you create new characters. Gradually, each player becomes more human while keeping aspects of the original animal. Explore how you can develop characters with animal-like traits. A mousy person might be timid, and alternate between freezing still and darting around the room. A lion might lazily sit around, but become ferocious when bothered. What does it really mean for someone to be "bull-headed?"

Part IV

Problem-Solving

In improvisation, we're constantly problem-solving. Whether you're playing comedic games, dramatic monoscenes, or anything in between, similar problems arise in telling stories. Some are technical, such as *How do we show action taking place in two different locations?* Some are existential, such as *"This scene is tanking—what the heck do we do now?"* Most of the time, caught up in the flow of experience, we solve these problems without consciously thinking about them.

Sometimes, though, we fall victim to the improviser's greatest fear: running out of ideas. It's our equivalent of the writer staring at a blank page, straining to get down words that just won't come. I've experienced these feelings in both professions, and it's never pleasant.

Of course, the concept is absurd. Your brain never stops thinking, and ideas are always there. In those moments where you feel at a loss, it's ego that's gotten in the way. Either you're judging your ideas too harshly or you're caught in the fear of being judged by others. In both cases, you're thinking about *you* and not the scene.

As I've mentioned many times now, environment work helps you escape this by redirecting your focus outward. It deflects the ego, gets you out of your head, and lets ideas rise to the surface. In this part of the book, we'll explore ways of turning to the environment when you feel stuck.

It's important to remember that these are not "*if this happens, then do this*" solutions. No single technique will work for every improviser in every situation. My goal is to expand your ability to get past yourself and land on an idea. One idea is all you ever need to continue the improvisation.

You Will Learn

- ways to discover *any* type of idea from the environment, such as character, relationship, conflict, emotional reactions, and more;
- how to proceed when you get a tricky environment suggestion or a scene takes an unexpected turn; and
- some easy staging effects for specific physical situations.

11

Making Discoveries from Environment

For me, learning improvised storytelling was a process of building instincts for what a scene needs. When I started out, my instructors would often side-coach with questions to help me make choices: *"Where are you?" "Who is that person?" "What does your character want?"* Over time, I learned to ask questions myself to advance a scene. These days, I don't consciously ask those questions. I get a *feeling* that something is missing, and make a choice to fill in that information.

I don't know your training background, or how your mind works, but I suspect similar instincts guide your improvisation. You don't know where you are, so you start an activity. You don't know who that person is, so you give them a name and a relationship. You feel directionless, so you give yourself an objective. And so on.

As you become aware of these instincts, you will often know what kind of offer you want to make, but may be stuck for what to do. In this chapter, we'll look at ways to discover ideas from objects and environment. I've hinted at ways to discover offers throughout the book so far. Here I'll be more specific, breaking down various types and providing exercises to help develop your instincts and reactions.

Even if you don't know what you need, patiently exploring the Where will always connect you to something you can use. Remember that this isn't simply jumping around the stage fiddling with objects. It's a process of observing your relationship to the environment and building on what you notice. The object work itself doesn't generate ideas; it's the open curiosity you do it with. (Review Chapter 6 if you want a refresher.)

Discovery and Reaction

Perhaps the most basic way to drive a scene is to simply observe and react.

In their must-read book *Process: An Improviser's Journey*, Mary Scruggs and Michael Gellman describe this discovery and reaction as a *Point of Concentration*. They propose three sources of discovery: objects, the environment, and other players. (Funnily enough, the book you're reading now happens to cover two of those sources.)

The idea in Point of Concentration is to make discoveries without "playwriting." Instead of figuring out how you can use an object, stay present and experience it until you discover something. Then have a *physical reaction* to your experience. The reaction doesn't have to be big, but it should be noticeable by everyone; otherwise your partner and the audience have nothing to see or work with.

Suppose you pick up a baseball. As you turn it around in your hands, you discover it's got a large scuff on one side. What is your reaction? You may be shocked, or sad, or thrilled. And you may express that feeling through a facial expression, a sound, or dialogue expressing your point of view— anything that shows the discovery has affected the character.

In Point of Concentration, this is ALL you do. Your reaction is the offer. You don't get ahead of yourself and decide this is your priceless Hank-Aaron-autographed baseball, and you're angry because your kid has wrecked it. Don't tell a story about the ball. Just have a reaction, and work with your partner from there.

Here again is the need for clear, specific object work. Your partner may not know exactly what you've discovered, but they need to understand the source of your reaction. If all they see is you frowning at an undefined *something* in your hand, it will be harder for them to work with that offer. Maybe you toss the ball in the air and turn it around in your hands first.

Discovery and reaction is best for long-form, slow-burn improv where you're exploring behavior rather than driving narrative. Scruggs and Gellman argue that heightening discoveries without playwriting is the only way to sustain a scene longer than five minutes. Their work is not about deliberately making choices.

That said, your reaction is always up to you. In short-form, you may want to make a narrative choice to tell a strong story quickly. Regardless of the way you improvise, your next action can always be motivated by making a discovery from an object or conditions in the environment.

My concern with Point of Concentration work is that it seems strongly based in visualization, which can be challenging as we discussed in Chapter 7. It might be easier to use this technique at the top of a scene when establishing a Where.

Throw an Environmental Curveball

Anytime you want to make discoveries, it's easiest to return to objects or environmental details you've already established instead of creating new ones. This can give those details more dramatic importance.

If you really want to shake things up, though, you can experiment with what Mick Napier[1] calls a *curveball*. At any time in a scene, without a preconceived idea, reach out and grab *something*. Just close your hand around an object without knowing what it is. Now continue the scene with that object in your hands. Eventually you will discover what it is and how it relates to the scene.

This is the improv illusionist's equivalent of a thrilling escape trick. It changes your energy and pushes your inspiration to new places. Observers will probably not even know what's happening. But the mysterious object will draw their attention.

As always, detail is your friend here. You don't know what the thing is, but you can still note your physicality and make choices. How are you holding it? Is it heavy? Move it around—does it ping your muscle memory in any way?

---

[1] Cofounder of the Annoyance Theater, director for multiple Second City revues, author of *Improvise* and *Behind the Scenes*.

Also pay attention to consistency. You might put the object down, or it may be fixed in place somewhere. When you return to it, it should be in the same place and handled the same way. (Don't wimp out and drop it—push yourself to discover!)

Whether or not you come to a decision about what this object is, it doesn't have to be a focus of the scene. Most often, it will either support or reveal something new about your character. Why is the president spinning a yo-yo while discussing foreign affairs? Who knows? But it tells you something interesting about them.

This is scary, no doubt, but it's a fun challenge. It's especially great if you're jaded about object work, or feeling you have to do things the "right" way all the time. With attention to detail and a sense of play, you'll learn to trust that ideas do suggest themselves.

Character and Personality

Activities reveal all sorts of things about who you are. I once saw an excellent example of this when introducing routines[2] to a workshop class. We picked the activity of pumping gasoline into a car. One of the first steps in the routine was opening the tank. From this single action, students made unique choices that led to interesting characters.

One student made very specific choices about the *object*. He established a very old car, where the gas cap was in the center of the rear bumper, and he was very careful removing it. Building on that physicality, he also noticed a smudge on the car's paint job and buffed it gently with his sleeve. It became clear he was a vintage car owner, very concerned about keeping everything in tip-top shape. Later, he admitted he first thought the car was old and rusty, but buffing the smudge changed his mind and gave more definition to his character's habits and personality.

Another student used the given *location* to start with a character choice. Thinking about who might be present at a gas station, she decided she was a worker instead of a car owner. As she opened the gas tank she called out, *"Fill 'er up today, sir?"* Her routine became about doing all the jobs of a full service gas attendant.

Here we can see that environment often suggests not only broad character *types*, but also character *traits* through the way they behave with the objects.

---

[2] See Chapter 4.

Small energy[3] actions are useful here. Choosing to buff a smudge is mundane behavior, but exploring it can tell you about who you are. Do you see another smudge, and then another, until you become obsessed? Do you use your sleeve, or must you use a special cloth you carry for these occurrences? Different characters emerge from small choices.

Another example: some newer cars have capless gas tanks, so in your routine, it might only be a matter of flipping open the cover panel. What energy do you bring to that small action? If you do it quickly, is your character in a hurry, or annoyed at something? If you do it slowly, why would that be? Are they planning to gas-and-dash? Do they find gasoline smelly and gross? (See all these different character *attitudes*?)

You can also decide to break the routine—maybe the cover falls off. Does this happen all the time, or did they just buy a faulty car? What *emotions* might that cause?

Even a single body movement can give you character ideas. Maybe you notice your arm did a weird thing. If you lean into that, it may change how you do the activity, which gives you something else to notice. These observations flow together, bringing a character into clearer focus.

Showing Who through the Use of Objects

Three players decide on a group of characters or a simple relationship, for example, scientists, cleaners, guard/prisoners, tourists/guide. Then, through the use of one or more objects, show the audience who those characters are. Afterward, discuss the specific objects or actions that clearly communicated information.

I sometimes combine this exercise with *Noting Your Physicality* (in the Exercises Appendix) to help players develop characters from the environment. Here they show not only the character types but also individual personalities.

Relationship and Dynamic

First, a quick refresher on what these terms mean. *Relationship* refers to the objective connection between characters: siblings, coworkers, doctor/

---

[3] See Chapter 8.

patient, and firefighter/kitten-in-a-tree are all examples. *Dynamic* refers to their subjective interaction, how they relate to each other. This could include personality, emotional reactions, status, and other factors affecting the relationship. The dynamic between two friendly coworkers might change if they learn they're competing for a promotion.

The easiest way to make a relationship choice from environment is to decide what type of people are natural to that place. Domestic locations suggest family/friend relationships. Office locations suggest professional/business relationships. You can be creative, but also don't be afraid to make the obvious choice. If a simple choice helps advance the scene faster, then by all means make it.

If all the characters fit the location, it's a great way to introduce a collaborative dynamic, where everyone works together on a common objective. This avoids the frequent problem of scenes devolving into arguments. "Peas in a pod" scenes work this way—you can start one by creating similar characters who fit the environment.

You can also ask who *doesn't* fit, like a vegan at a burger joint, or a priest in jail. This creates dynamic tension even if characters are working together—they will naturally have different approaches to the objective. When a character doesn't fit the place, it's a good starting point for a "fish out of water" or "ordinary character, extraordinary world" scene.

Another way to play with dynamic is to adjust your physical alignment with other characters. For example, imagine a scene with two scientists. The relationship suggests equality, and we expect their physical behavior to be *aligned*. They'll use their equipment and treat their lab in similar ways. Any conflict or problem will likely come from outside the relationship, and these two will handle it together. (I wish more scenes were like this.)

You can add a new dimension to this relationship by *misaligning* your physicality. Suppose one scientist is sloppy and careless with the experiments. What does that suggest? Are they new to the lab? Are they days from retirement and don't care anymore? Now you have Boss Scientist/New Scientist, or Jaded Scientist/Idealist Scientist. The new relationship can then suggest status or attitudes to play, even if the characters aren't in conflict.

This exploration can also happen the opposite way, where you make a relationship/dynamic choice *first,* and then enhance it with a physical choice. If a high/low status emerges, you can start to misalign your activity to express that dynamic. With both partners grounded in the environment, it's easy to spot opportunities to do this.

Aligned/Misaligned Relationship

Two players choose a relationship and an activity they can do together. Throughout the scene they handle objects related to the activity. Observe each other and handle objects the same way (aligned). At some point, the coach calls out *"Shift!"* and the players now handle objects in different ways of their choosing (misaligned).

Talk about how the relationship and dynamic appear to change, even if the characters change nothing else about their behavior.

Conflict

Conflict is the obstacles or challenges preventing characters from getting what they want. Narrative is created from the characters' attempts to overcome these obstacles, where success is never guaranteed. An argument is an obvious (and overused) way to introduce conflict—each character sees the other as their obstacle. But arguments tend to be circular and don't resolve easily, which can kill a scene.[4] Environment often provides other sources of conflict.

Of course, a hostile environment presents plenty of obstacles, both minor and extreme. Characters usually have to work together to manage these environments, which is a great alternative to arguing. It's easy to think of such conflicts in outdoor scenes—everything from avalanches to zebra stampedes—but even indoor environments can turn hostile. Can you save dinner when it catches on fire? Will you finish that important office presentation when the power goes out?

You can also introduce objects to create a challenge for characters. It's harder for one roommate to ask another to move out if the second roommate is sharpening a machete. Getting through a locked door without the key is always a problem.

---

[4] Avoiding arguments is a common improv "rule," but characters can argue as long as you keep advancing the scene. If you do find yourself stalled, offering a compromise is one way to deflect an argument.

Objects can also be symbols of a character's inner conflict. An angry person, holding their tongue, may crush a wine glass or tear pages in a book. A yearning lover, unable to express themself, might twist the ring on their finger. So might a cheating spouse.

Another way to experiment with conflict is to establish a different environment than suggested by someone else's activity. For example, suppose one character is pushing a cart, hollering, *"Ice cream, get your ice cream!"* Then another player comes in and begins sorting books onto shelves, establishing a library. This isn't necessarily blocking the first improviser's idea. Instead, it creates a conflict for the ice cream vendor to sell their product in an unusual (and quiet) setting. Be very careful with offers like this, as they usually force a burden of justification on the scene (such as why the vendor is working inside the library). It's not polite to "serve up"[5] your fellow players like this unless they're ready for it.

Game of the Scene

Del Close[6] experimented with the idea that long-form scenes contain "games" that players discover, unlike most short-form improv where the game is imposed from the start. *Game of the scene* has since become an important concept in improv theory. It's especially central to the style of the Upright Citizens Brigade Theatre.

According to the UCB method, improvisers first establish a "base reality" for a scene with a Who, What, and Where. Then they watch for a "first unusual thing" that is out of sync with the base reality. This becomes the first event in a pattern of behavior that produces the scene's laughs. Once the players recognize a pattern and begin to deliberately explore it, we say they have "found the Game." Justifying, interpreting, and exploring that behavior is how you play the Game.[7]

---

[5] This is my replacement for the old-school improv term "pimping," which the community is trying to replace with more respectful language. It happens when one player forces another to do something difficult. Serving up a partner can be good fun if everyone is willing to play, but more often it's cruel behavior.

[6] Improv philosopher, controversial teacher/director, originator of the Harold, coauthor of *Truth in Comedy*.

[7] Mick Napier's definition is simpler: a Game is anything an improviser does that makes the audience say, *"I want to see them do more of that."*

Obviously, your physical improv skills will be useful in establishing any base reality. Later in the scene, you can often find a Game by playfully exploring the environment. Small energy movements or object permanence can be a source of patterns if they're played consistently by everyone.

When you establish *trouble*[8] with an object, and then others have the same trouble, it becomes a Game you can play. Imagine a room with a loose floorboard that everyone trips over. This can also lead to larger ideas about the characters—maybe they're generally clumsy, or maybe there's a reason they're stuck with this bad flooring. One character can also play *against* the Game—gracefully stepping over the floorboard—which changes their dynamic with the others.[9]

Note that this runs against the idea that Games should emerge organically. If you're always trying to force a Game, you will create patterns that lead to a lack of variety.

---

[8] See Chapter 3.
[9] Be careful that playing against the Game doesn't turn into blocking or cancelling an offer.

12

Three Elements: How to Handle Tricky Situations

Over my career, I've done hundreds of improv presentations in schools, and even more family-friendly gigs. Many performers I know hate these types of shows. Sometimes it's about having to watch our language and avoid taboo subjects. More often it's because of the audience suggestions. Kids get excited, and they love to yell stuff, and the stuff they yell sometimes doesn't make sense or is just weird.[1]

One night at Oakville Improv, James Jeffers and I made a snap-decision to do our next scene silently. James loves physical play as much as I do, so we

---

[1] Of course, we equally don't like adults who try to force performers into embarrassing situations. I've heard suggestions like *"a vibrator," "a proctologist's office,"* and *"porno actors"* more often than I care to remember. Kids are bizarrely creative. Adults love to provoke, but they're kind of lazy about it.

like to challenge ourselves once in a while. When we asked for a suggestion of a location, some kid yelled out *"the stomach of an ant!"* Challenge indeed.

James and I froze and looked at each other. We could see each other thinking the same thing: *how the hell are we going to do this, and with no dialogue?* Then the lights came up, and we just had to.

We collapsed down on top of each other and squeezed in. There was no way to discuss how we got into an ant's stomach, so the scene was simply about *getting out.* We pushed at the walls, and I found an orifice above us. I squeezed my way out—first a hand, then my head, then the rest of me—and stood up. Looking down, I picked up a tiny ant from the stage and stared at it in wonder.

Meanwhile, James was brilliant—still inside the ant, he matched every move of my hand as I tilted it, tumbling around inside. I put the ant down, pushed a finger inside, then my hand and arm. James grabbed on and I pulled him free. As the lights went down, I stomped on the little menace before anything nasty happened again.

Weird, right? But also a show-stopper, one of those scenes that seems to come direct from the improv gods. I'm sure that if we hadn't committed to silence, we'd have motor-mouthed our way into something much less captivating. We started completely in the unknown, and it was our attention to environment that saved us.

Since that day, I've been less inclined to dismiss children's ideas.

Tricky Situations

Taking suggestions is popular because it involves the audience in the show, and it also gives newer players a definitive place to start from. The drawback is *you're expected to use the idea you get,* even if it's confusing, offensive, or uninspiring. Rejecting it and asking for something else is always an option, but the next suggestion could be equally problematic. Being fussy starts to look bad—the audience wonders why you're asking for ideas if you don't want to use them.[2]

Suggestions aren't the only source of potential difficulty. Weird objects and environments can pop up anytime in a scene. A player points at you and screams, *"Ewww, a tarantula!"* Or maybe you've been doing office work when it's suddenly revealed you're in the middle of the jungle.

---

[2] One way to manipulate a tough suggestion is to use it as inspiration for something else. It can help to describe your thinking (*"You know, 'toilet plunger' makes me think of my grandfather . . ."*), but you can lose the audience if they suspect you're trying to evade them.

Sometimes you get stuck, not knowing how to show what's going on. Sometimes you get an idea, but then find your scene partners aren't reading what you're doing. And *then* you get stuck, repeating that same movement slower and harder like a tortured game of charades. Blanking like this can throw you up into your head, and that's when panic starts.

In tricky situations, we want to generate a new choice fast, commit to it, and get back into the flow of the scene. In this chapter, I'll share an easy technique that's helped me with this throughout my career.

The "Modern Family" Drill

In my first show for The Second City Touring Company, our Act 1 closer was an improv game called "Modern Family." (This was long before the TV sitcom of the same name.) It started with a short scene featuring the members of a family coming and going through the house, each making jokes referencing the news and pop culture of the day. After that, we'd ask the audience for an earlier decade in the twentieth century, then redo the same scene, changing the jokes to fit events from the suggested time period. Then we'd do it a third time for an even earlier decade.

Our director, Shari Hollett, wanted us to play this as a real improv game instead of preparing and re-using gags for each possible decade. She challenged us to read up on twentieth-century history and use different ideas every time. In rehearsals, we would drill this by choosing a random decade, and then everyone would try to call out three historical events before running the scene. The game was to choose one and try to make a joke out of it.

As I worked at this, I discovered it was actually easier to come up with jokes when I had three events to choose from than if I had only one. I also began to realize I could do this *anytime* I was stumped for an idea. And it was especially effective for object work and environments.

The Power of Three

Three is a big number in human psychology. Our brains are wired to recognize patterns, and three is the smallest number of elements it takes to establish one. When you have two elements, you naturally start to anticipate what the third item will be. If the third bit confirms your anticipation, it's a satisfying experience. The brain is very comfortable with groups of three.

A lot of comedy uses the Rule of Three: setup, build, punchline. Usually, the punchline goes against anticipation, which surprises and makes you laugh.[3] In improv, I've found that *confirming* a pattern can sometimes work just as well. It makes the audience feel smart, because you're completing a thought they've had themselves.

Pattern recognition explains why sometimes your partners can't read your activity. If you drop to all fours and crawl around the stage, you're only giving them one bit of information. You could be doing that for any number of reasons. If you also start panting and wagging your tail, then the three elements together complete a pattern and they see you as a dog. Thinking in threes helps you communicate more specific detail.

Here's an exercise to help you start thinking this way:

Three Person Tableau

Players stand in a circle. Player 1 enters the circle and poses as a statue, declaring what they are; for example, *"I'm a tree."* Player 2 adds to the picture as a complementary feature of the first object; for example, *"I'm a bird in the tree."* Player 3 adds another complementary feature; for example, *"I'm a cowering worm."* Once you have three, Player 1 chooses one of the other two statues to remain while the others clear. Start again with that statue.

Most of the time, I talk about going with your *first* idea. Following one idea keeps things simple and is usually the best approach. In a tricky situation, when you're stuck and don't know how to move forward, thinking in threes can kickstart your intuition. You pick your favorite idea of the three and go with that. You then have two more ideas to layer on if the first one isn't getting across.

Here's how to do it.

---

[3] An example from standup comedian Laura Kightlinger: *"I can't think of anything worse after a night of drinking than waking up next to someone and not being able to remember their name, or how you met, or why they're dead."*

The Three Elements Technique

Let's keep using the same example of playing a dog. It may seem simple, but any improviser can get stuck on any idea at any time. For our purposes here, let's suppose you need to play a dog and are blanking on how to do it.

Quick as you can, think of *three elements* of a dog you would use to describe it to someone else. These can be *anything* that comes to mind. They could be:

- a basic feature (four legs, a tail, floppy ears);
- a behavior (jumps up on people, yappy bark, panting with its tongue out);
- a specific quirk (eats messily, sleeps on its back); or
- what you do with it (walk it on a leash, stroke its fur).

Your elements could be based on a specific dog you know, or the general concept. They don't have to be unique to dogs, or even objectively accurate. They're whatever you think of when you think "dog."

Some people do this by thinking of one element and then free-associating to add two more. For example, you might think of the tail, and then that leads you to the tail wagging, and then to an excited dog jumping up on people. But the elements don't have to be related to each other.

Don't overthink or judge—you need an idea fast, and obvious ideas are just as good as anything else. It shouldn't take more than a couple of seconds to come up with three elements for a dog.

Now that you have three, pick any one and go. Use that element to make the dog visible in the scene, whether as an improvised object or by becoming the dog as a character.

Suppose I come up with these elements:

1. panting tongue;
2. four legs; and
3. lifts its leg and pees on stuff (a cheap gag, but I'm not judging myself!).

The four-legs idea stands out to me, so I start with that. I'd drop to the stage and start crawling around. Given the scene context, this may be enough for my partners to understand and work with me.

If things go well, I may be further inspired by the elements I've chosen, or my partners may react in a way that moves things forward. If we're all still stuck, I don't have to stand there helpless. I can bring out the panting tongue, and/or start lifting my leg on stuff. The three elements together are more likely to complete a pattern for my partners, helping them recognize what I'm doing.

Whichever element you start with, you still have two more to layer on. This helps you fill in more detail and enhance the scene. It also keeps you from mindlessly repeating a single element, which doesn't help.

Again, that's a very simple example, which seems like a lot of work for little payoff. But now let's try something trickier, like being endowed as that tarantula. In thinking about how to show an eight-limbed creature when you only have four, you might find yourself stuck. So, come up with three elements, then pick one and go. You then have two others as layer-ons. Here's what I think of:

1. moves slowly, one leg at a time;
2. crawls up walls; and
3. spins a web (technically not true, but it still communicates the idea of a *spider*—don't overthink it!).

Maybe I'd start by flattening myself against a wall, then slowly climbing up. I could then try to spin a line and creep along it. Moving in a slow, deliberate way, I may be able to create the impression of having eight legs. It's a fun challenge! It might not work, but at least I've found a way to keep the scene moving, instead of freezing in panic over how to play a giant spider.

Remember this isn't a fixed method. You never have to stick with your three elements. If a better idea pops up, or the scene redirects somewhere more interesting, follow that.

Three Elements Pinball

I created this exercise as a drill to practice quickly generating three specific details for any audience suggestion: object, location, activity, character, relationship, genre, or emotion.

Players stand in a circle, using an improvised basketball. Player 1 passes to anyone, calling out a category from the list above, for example, *"Location!"* Player 2 passes to anyone, providing the suggestion, for example, *"An office!"* Player 3 holds the ball while they call out three elements of that suggestion, for example, *"Desk! Computer! Loud co-worker!"* Any elements related to the suggestion are fine—they don't have to be original. We're looking for speed. When finished, Player 3 passes to anyone, and the cycle starts over.

Encourage spontaneity to keep the ball moving fast. Also, keep an eye on the consistency of the ball. As players stop to think, they may lose focus and unconsciously change the object.

Once players get good at this, the coach can optionally stop them occasionally, getting the player to pick one of their three elements and start a scene.

Note that players 1 and 2 often find it just as challenging to select the category and example. This is a good illustration of why we need to think in advance about the suggestions we'll want to ask for in a show.

You can also think in *groups* of threes. A *Specialized Where* scene combines settings to put a new spin on things, like an office in the jungle. If you found yourself stuck for how to do that, you could start by thinking of three elements for each:

- jungle: gorilla, banana trees, vines;
- office: commute, phone calls, co-worker;

And then smash them together to get some fun potential ideas for the scene:

1. commute to work—via swinging vine;
2. answering phone calls—on a banana-phone (peel it to answer?); or
3. friendly co-worker—who is a gorilla.

This is more challenging, but it's an effective way of turning *thinking* back into *action*.

The Specialized Where

Players get a generic location, for example, office, classroom, kitchen. Then they decide on a more specific setting to show the audience, for example, swamp office, outer-space classroom, a kitchen in Hell. They can agree in advance on Who they are and What they're doing.

Of course you can experiment, but this is usually best played by carrying out the common activities of the generic location, layering on the added perspective of the unusual setting.

Three at Once

I've suggested the idea of *"choose one element and go"* for simplicity—you only ever need one idea to get back on track. You don't always have to use your elements in one—two—three progression, though. For common objects, it's easy to show all the elements at once. You might create the dog on all fours with the panting tongue and leg-lifting all together. That's great— your activity has detail and you can continue to heighten and explore your choice. When you're completely stumped, starting with one element and then adding more can help you work your way into it.

The reality is that you already use combined elements all the time. If you pick up an improvised cup and drink from it, you're showing us at least three elements of that cup: it fits in your hand, there's liquid inside, and you sip from it. The pattern is immediately apparent. It's the *specifics* of the elements that are important. To show you're drinking coffee, you hold a mug handle, sip it carefully, and enjoy the aroma. If it's whiskey, you pinch a shot glass, slug it back, and grimace at the burn. Now imagine how the secret alcoholic who's carrying whiskey in their coffee mug would do it. From similar elements, you can create distinctly different objects and behaviors.

The extra ideas you generate are there for you to use *if needed*. You never have to put every detail into your performance.

Finding Elements in Research

In Chapter 9, when we talked about researching real-world objects, places, and activities, you may have wondered if there are *specific* details you should look for to reproduce in your improv.

Now that you know the Three Elements technique, you have a framework for observing details. Notice the *common elements* for objects or environments of the same type (e.g., most cars have seats with seat belts), and the *distinct elements* that make something unique (e.g., a Formula 1 car has only one seat with a harness). Thinking deliberately about this makes it easier to bring elements to mind later, without relying on visualization.

It's also easier to think of *different* elements on the spot, instead of the same clichéd three. This adds variety to your performance, so you're not playing the same type of peeing dog all the time.

Bonus: Use It for Any Idea

Three elements works for more than just objects, locations, and activities. It works for ANY tricky situation. Here are some examples of suggestions you might get, and three quick elements I thought up for each.

- Genre—Film Noir: smoking, drinking, stilted narration
- Character—Scientist: safety goggles, lab coat, notebook
- Relationship—Siblings: taunting, stealing toys, complaining to Mom
- Emotion—Nervous: wringing hands, glancing around, tugging ear

What elements do you come up with? How would you play them?

Remember that this technique is only meant as a quick idea generator to get you out of your head and back into the flow of a scene. I don't recommend you use it as a regular procedure. Like researching elements themselves, it's something you need to think about offstage so it comes to mind when you need it. Take regular time for thought experiments. Give yourself tricky suggestions and ask, "*What are the elements here?*"

Weird ideas will never catch you off-guard again.

13

Physical Stage Effects

Active, dynamic improv sometimes raises unique staging problems, like how to show simultaneous action in two different locations, or how to play characters standing above or below each other. This chapter is a collection of physical techniques for creating these effects. Practice them with your team so you can get feedback on how they look before you break them out in performance.

Beware that while they're huge fun to play with, these can be a little gimmicky and shouldn't be overused.

Camera Angles and Perspective

I've recommended you study movies and TV to research environmental detail. They're also great for exploring *camera angles*. Film uses a wide variety of shots and camera placements to control what the director wants you to see. By imagining the audience viewpoint as the camera, you can orient yourself to simulate these effects.

One example is the *close-up*, which brings us deep into the experience of the subject. You can bring the character closer to the audience by turning your full face forward and stepping downstage. Monologues and asides often use this technique, although you don't have to step out of the scene. A distraught lover can face outward, revealing emotion the other character doesn't see. Take care to avoid breaking eye contact with your partner for too long.

If you have one, a spotlight also focuses attention like a close-up. Your lighting improviser can watch for you to hit a stage marker under the spot. For maximum effect, other players should step out of the light as it comes on.

Try unusual angles. Bedroom scenes are sometimes filmed from above the bed, looking down on the characters. To recreate this camera angle, picture it as if the mattress is standing on end, perpendicular to the stage. By standing in front of it, it looks like you're "lying" on the bed.[1]

Play around with *perspective*. Imagine you're playing Godzilla. You could act as if tiny people are scurrying around under your feet, but isn't it more fun to see other players use their wiggling fingers to show us the frightened humans?

I once saw a freaky scene with the perspective of distance. While one player stood at the front of the stage, another was at the very back, using his finger as a puppet for a far-away character. "Hey, wait up!" he called, in a tiny voice, then started moving forward. As he got closer, the finger puppet became a hand, then an arm. He "grew" to full size by the time he arrived at the front of the stage, breathless from the running. Then he realized he'd forgotten something and ran back the same way, "shrinking" in the distance!

Another way to change the audience's viewpoint is to make them look around. Use the whole theatre. Enter and exit scenes through the audience. Have characters appear among or behind them. A narrator in this position can easily direct attention to something specific on the stage. (Be careful when moving through the audience, especially in the dark. Keep everyone safe!)

Split-Screens

You've likely seen movies where two people are chatting on the phone, with the frame split so you see them both at once. This is easy to replicate if you make it clear that two parts of the stage are different locations.

---

[1] In one such bedroom scene at The Second City, a character dropped a real prop on the stage, which according to an above-the-bed camera angle would have meant it had shot out of his hand across the room. To which another character replied: *"Shut the window, it's really windy in here!"*

Players outside or inside the scene can introduce a split-screen. From outside, a player slides in from the side of the stage, claiming the space around them. On exiting, they slide out again and release the space. From inside the scene, a player can exit the current location but remain on stage as they enter a new environment. This often happens when a character has to fetch something from the next room.

Be careful about *entrances* when creating a split-screen. Players on stage may assume you're joining them where they are. A narrative statement can help. As you enter you might say, *"At the same time, in a hotel room across town . . ."* Notice that you don't say *"Meanwhile . . ."* That word usually signals a complete change of scene—the other players will clear the stage, and you won't get the intended split-screen. Your team can set up and practice signals that work for you.

Heighten the reality of a split-screen by staying aware of the distance between the two locations. Obviously, if they're far away from each other, the characters won't be able to interact without a phone or other communication device. (Maybe telepathy?) If you're closer, but in different rooms, you have to call out to each other, even though you're in reality only a few feet away. Characters in different places also can't see each other (although the improvisers still observe everything that's going on).

Always be aware of keeping space between the two locations, and be careful not to cross the "split line," which will confuse everyone!

Levels and Climbing

Stories don't always happen on a flat plane. Play with *levels* where characters are in the same location but above or below each other. How do we show Romeo serenading Juliet on her balcony if the actors are both standing on the same stage floor?

This is a specialized kind of split-screen, which you make more believable through the direction each player faces. Each looks toward where the other *would be* instead of directly at them. Obviously, a character who is higher up will look down, and those below will look up. The more you match body and head angles with your partner, the better.

I don't recommend you play this way for very long. It forces you to break eye contact, which degrades your scene work. Look for reasons to get back onto the same level as soon as you can.

You can also play with traveling between levels. There are lots of options: stairs, ladders, ropes, trees, and anything else you can "climb" up or down. As you climb, straighten or bend your body to add the visual impression of going up or down. When climbing up, reach above you to put your hand on the space where the ledge is, and "pull" it down to the floor so that you're standing on it. When climbing down, you might add a little trouble finding the bottom with your foot before the last step. Or you could "drop" the last few inches by giving a little hop.

As a scene partner, you can help by adjusting distance and head angle as the person climbs toward or away from you. This also creates space for the split-screen effect.

Changing Locations—The "Revolving Door"

We tend to assume that the stage is one location. That doesn't mean you have to stay in that place. Suppose all the characters want to move into the next room. In this situation, someone usually places a door in the middle of the stage. Everyone walks through, and we assume the location has changed.

It's a convenient shortcut, but it breaks the visual reality. If the players have already been using the whole stage, the appearance of the new door is confusing. And you don't want to give up half the stage just in case you need space for another room.

A fancier way to do this is to place the doorway at the edge of the stage, and then turn in a tight circle as you enter the next room. It's almost as if you're going through a revolving door. You "emerge" into a new, blank space. Of course, everyone has to follow along with you for this effect to work. If any of the characters are staying in the previous room, they'll have to clear the stage in the opposite direction, or collapse the space down to a small split-screen.

You can make a game of this if you find ways to go back and forth between rooms, or keep moving forward into new ones. It's also fun to remember the different layouts and return to objects in the various rooms as you come and go.

Real Estate Tour

This exercise is excellent for experimenting with split-screens, levels, and changing locations. Play a scene where one player, a real estate agent, leads other players on a home tour. Move through different rooms, go up and down stairs, and play with objects in each room. Maybe a player lingers in one room while the rest of the group moves on. How well can you establish and remember the layout of the house?

Part V

Safety

After promoting the value of environment work to improvisation, my second main goal with this book is to increase awareness of performer safety. These goals are linked, because physical play increases safety risk. Even so, we should always remember the potential for physical and emotional harm regardless of how you improvise.

Changing attitudes is a key first step of this process. If you drop a question about physical injuries into any community discussion, you'll hear dozens of stories about everything from scrapes and bruises to concussions and broken limbs. These are often shared as amusing anecdotes, as if it's *"just part of the gig."* Respectfully, I disagree. All injuries are serious and preventable.

And while excellent work has been done to promote emotional safety in recent years, these aren't new issues either. They're highly pervasive and won't simply go away now that we're shining a light on them. For both Physical and Emotional Safety in improv, we need proactive attention from all members of the community. It seems paradoxical, but taking improv safety seriously will actually increase our freedom for creative play.

While some companies do publish their own policies and procedures, I've found few if any centralized resources for safety information. My ideas here are meant as a start toward creating one. I hope they amplify and inspire the work of more knowledgeable and influential improvisers.

You Will Learn

- some best practices for preventing physical injuries during shows, rehearsals, and workshops; and
- that emotional safety is an issue for *all* improvisers, and how Boundary Conversations and Consent Practice help create more open, safer improv spaces.

14

Physical Safety

Summer 2001. I was just starting my second year with The Second City Touring Company out of Toronto. We were booked for a week at a theatre in Quebec's beautiful Eastern Townships, only days after the birth of my first child. I'd much rather have been at home with my wife and baby, but professional acting gigs can be precarious, and I didn't feel I could take parental leave. In consolation, I was looking forward to spending the days touring the area, swimming, and enjoying the downtime.

On the night of our first show, we got a frantic phone call from the theatre. They'd given us the wrong call time, and we were late. We rushed in, but there was only enough time for a minimal tech rehearsal, and none to really explore the space. As we started the show, and I made my first entrance, I noticed the backdrop curtains were too long, and they bunched up on the floor. But there was no time to do anything about it.

The opening scene was followed by a blackout gag that called for me to sprint off stage. As I did, my left foot caught the curtain and rolled. Within minutes, my ankle swelled to double its size and I could barely put weight on it. But the show must go on. In the first intermission, I wrapped my foot and downed a few painkillers. I made it through.

We still had a week of shows to do, and being far from home, no understudies were available. To be able to do the show every night, I spent every day resting in our cabin. Our non-air-conditioned cabin. Alone with my thoughts of home and family, while the rest of my cast got out and about.

Not. Fun.

Safety Imperatives

Improv lets you create amazing stories without innate danger. You can spend hours underwater without drowning. Improvised pyrotechnics won't set your hair on fire. You can duel to the death, and no one dies.

However, make no mistake: *ALL performance is dangerous, and unrehearsed, spontaneous acting is even more so.* With improv, you have no pre-set blocking or choreography to rely on. You're negotiating entrances, exits, and stairs in low (or no) light. Tripping over chairs, curtains, and other players is a constant threat. Committing to more physicality makes it especially important to be aware of these hazards.

This chapter is full of safety tips I've learned, some the hard way. It's not a complete list, and there may be other factors unique to your situation. If you belong to an improv company, check for published safety policies and warnings. (Every company should have these.) If you're a bar-prov troupe, in a different place every night, elect someone to ask the venue management about safety issues.

ALL performers must take responsibility for *three safety imperatives* at all times:

1. play safely;
2. protect others (players and audience); and
3. protect yourself.

Controlled Commitment

Throughout this book, we've seen how to mesmerize audiences with physicality and attention to environment. To do this well, you have to commit to using as much energy and movement as the scene calls for. Whether it's a thrilling mountaintop rescue or the misadventures of a new puppy, you have to be ready to go for it.

That said, playing safe means *staying in physical control at all times*. Adrenaline, stage nerves, and audience response can all push you into dangerous actions. Be aware of this in advance and listen to your body. If you feel out of control, you ARE out of control. Slow down. Breathe.

Know your limits, and be ready to pass on an idea if it doesn't feel safe. Ninja cartwheels are an awesome spectacle, but they have no place in the show if you're going to sprain a wrist or fall into the audience. Remember also the warnings about muscle strains from our introduction to object work in Chapter 3.

Maybe you don't think this is a big deal. You accept the risks and want the added energy to boost your show. Even so, consider that the audience cares about your safety. When a performer *looks* unsafe, they will focus on the danger and not the show. This is not the result you want, any more than you want to injure yourself.

So, commit 100 percent to your scene, but commit equally to playing safe!

Situational Awareness

A blank improv stage can actually be *more* dangerous than a fully stocked theatre set. The open space creates false assumptions about freedom of movement. As a result, you're likely to be going faster when you hit that stray chair, another player, or the lip of the stage. Constant awareness of what's going on around you is essential.

All players develop a "third eye" for what an improvisation needs. You use it all the time when deciding to enter a scene, make an edit, or even position yourself on the backline. Situational awareness is also important for spotting and fixing hazards that pop up throughout a show.

Environment work really helps with this. It causes you to naturally glance around the stage and see what's happening. If a player enters, you see them.

If you notice a chair that wasn't cleared from the last scene, you can move it (and make sure everyone sees you do it). Find reasons in the scene to turn and monitor all 360 degrees.

Use your peripheral vision. If someone is sneaking up on your character, you may not want to look at them directly. However, you the *improviser* should always know what they're up to. Play away from them, but avoid fully turning your back.

Take a moment now to think about your recent scene work. Do you bump into furniture or people a lot? Are you surprised to find players have entered your scenes without you noticing? If so, you need to work on your situational awareness.

One good safety habit is to *always clear the stage of furniture and physical props with every scene change*. Resetting the stage picture is also a visual cue that a new scene is starting.

Walk the Stage

Over the course of a career, you will perform in dozens, maybe hundreds of different venues, many of which weren't built for improv. But even if you're always on the same controlled stage, you should check for hazards before every show. While stage managers and venue personnel should do this, it's a good idea to also do it yourself. You're the one in danger if someone else misses something.

Before the audience comes in, take a few minutes to walk the stage. Look for danger spots: loose floor panels, debris, water spills, and so on. Point out anything unusual to your stage manager and keep tabs on what's done to fix it.

Check furniture for loose screws or wobbling. You should be confident that all chairs or boxes will support your weight, sitting or standing. If not, take them completely offstage so that no one accidentally grabs them later.

Try to anticipate problems. One time on tour, our stage was in the main hall of a village community center. It was four wooden risers, set onto plastic milk crates, on a smooth tile floor. In the middle of a dance number, the crates shifted and the stage cracked open like an earthquake movie. If we'd thought about that in advance, we might have asked the venue to take out the milk crates, or even done the show on the floor.

Walking the stage also helps to refresh your spatial memory. Learn the number of steps from the entrances to front and center stage. If you're forced to enter in the dark, you'll want to keep your steps well below that number.

On that point, you should ONLY be moving around in a full blackout if the stage edges and all furniture are well-marked with glow tape. If you're touring or attending a makeshift venue, your group should keep a roll handy and mark the stage as necessary.

If a lighting technician is present, ask them to show you the various light cues: washes, spotlights, and blackouts. Look for shadows that might be an issue. And if you're not confident of your safety in the dark, ask for a low-level wash between scenes instead.

A quick walk-through should be standard practice before every show, even if you're in a regular run on the same stage. If anything around you seems out of place, or gives you a bad vibe, speak up!

Fitness

In playing the reality of an improvised world, your body may be put to the test. If there's a marathon, you might be running in place for several minutes. If you're playing a frog prince, you might be crouching and hopping. Add in some performance adrenaline and you can quickly run up against your physical limits.

A basic level of fitness is necessary for actors. You don't have to be a distance runner, a yogi, or a gym rat. Just try to get your heart rate up regularly. Fitness also helps your body deal better with stress, which lessens nerves before a show and helps you come down from the excitement afterwards.

Regular stretching is also beneficial. I have low flexibility, and long ago I'd get serious hip cramps almost every time I was on stage. I now stretch for 10 minutes most mornings and have far fewer problems.

Protect your voice, especially if you're playing more than once a week. Learn to breathe from the diaphragm, and use plenty of air to support your vocal projection. Drink lots of water to hydrate your throat.

Warm up, stretch, and breathe before every show or workshop. Your body and brain need oxygen to be fully alert—not only for safety but to allow your best ideas to flow.

Acrobatic moves are spectacular, but take a moment to consider your ability. I've known many performers (including myself) to strain muscles or tweak their back. It's rarely serious, but why take the risk? Hurting yourself for the audience's benefit isn't worth it. You're an improviser, not a gladiator.

Always check yourself for injuries after a show. It's amazing what you don't feel while the adrenaline is pumping. Don't wait until you wake up in pain the next day to start treating an injury.

Alcohol and Drugs

I'll keep this short because it should be obvious. Performing drunk or high is very risky. Alcohol and drugs compromise both your situational awareness and your reaction time. They also lower your inhibitions, which may help with stage anxiety, but also push you to actions beyond safe boundaries. If you're not in control, you're a danger to yourself and others. Celebrate or commiserate *after* the show.

Speaking of which, beware of risks in the social atmosphere around improv. In my career, I've heard too many horrible stories about the short- and long-term effects of alcohol, drugs, and partying: health problems, lost jobs, physical and sexual assault, arrests, addiction, early death. I am by no means against safe drinking or legal drug use, and I love a good after-party. I just want you to be safe.

Finally, if you ever feel you "need" a drink or a hit to be able to improvise, that's a huge red flag you must address.

Clothing

It's not my place to judge your style, but the clothes you wear to perform do have an effect on the audience. It should be a conscious choice, either to fit the tone of your show or at least to avoid distractions. "Smart casual" looks more professional and makes a wider range of characters believable. It doesn't feel right when an actor plays an uptight CEO while wearing a graphic t-shirt and flip-flops. It's also disrespectful to a crowd that's giving their time and money for an evening of entertainment.

Clothing choice is also a safety issue. Loose or restricting clothes can cause problems for physical actors. Above all, you should be able to move around comfortably. Look for stretch fabrics—they help prevent split seams and tears.

Be mindful of anything that could snag or get caught on a passing improviser. Avoid bulky jewelry and empty your pockets. You'll also want to protect your skin from abrasions and "furniture bites," especially your knees. I don't recommend you perform or rehearse in shorts.

Footwear is most important. The safest shoes enclose your whole foot and cover your toes. Platforms, heels, sandals, and slides all have their own particular dangers.

A tip I learned for those who wear dresses, skirts, or kilts: wear bike shorts underneath, or at least underwear with more coverage. You can commit to a wider range of movement while protecting your modesty.

Again, be aware of *looking* unsafe. If the audience is worried your shoes could fly off, or that you're about to split your pants, they're not paying attention to the story.

Lifts and Carries

This comes up more than you might expect. Besides moving furniture around the stage, you might also be moving your fellow players, like flying a superhero around, or carrying someone on your back.

The simple rule is, *if you're not 100 percent confident you can lift something or someone, DON'T.* Apart from dropping them, you risk straining your back or stumbling and falling.

It's worth asking players in advance about their comfort with being lifted, especially if you're working with someone new. That comfort can also change from day to day. Pre-show check-ins should be part of your routine. (See also Chapter 15 on Emotional Safety.)

Even if you've discussed it, never leap on someone or pick them up without a last-second check-in. Make eye contact and be sure they're ready. Ask for and get clear consent—it's not hard to work this into dialogue. When someone offers to carry me, I use a quick shoulder-tap as a signal I'm about to hop up.

You can also use an alternative to the piggyback that doesn't involve lifting at all. Put your hands on your partner's shoulders and get in close, with a little hop to look like you're mounting. Then the two of you move together, both with your feet on the floor.

If you do lift anything, remember to use your legs, with a wide base of support. Protect your back!

Violence

Inevitably, there will be improvisations where characters want to fight physically. This is especially dangerous if you haven't practiced for safety. Adrenaline runs high on stage, and if you don't maintain control it's easy to lash out unintentionally.

You can always find ways to avoid violence. But let's face it: the audience loves this stuff. Popular culture is full of punch-ups and shoot-outs, and some genres use violence as an established and expected narrative convention. So, let's discuss how to play it safely.

An IMPORTANT NOTE: I'm not a licensed fight instructor, and these are NOT official stage combat techniques. Ideally, every improviser should take a professional class at some point in their career.[1]

As much as I harp on playing the reality of a scene, staged violence is a major exception. Here are some basics.

1. *No force applied*

The first and most important principle is that the "victim" does all the work of creating the illusion of pain. The "attacker" never strikes or applies force— they simply support the illusion with appropriate body positioning.

2. *Keep your distance*

With true fight choreography, actors practice their moves close in to the body. Improv is much different. For safety, we need to stay well away from physical contact. If you're out of reach of the other player, you can't actually strike them, no matter how sloppy either of you might be.

---

[1] It can help to review one of many available books on fight choreography. A good one is *Combat Mime* by J.D. Martinez. However, remember that choreographed fighting illusions are different from improv. Such movements should still be done in slow-motion.

So, keep distance between you, and avoid stepping in to fight. This is difficult because the brain's instinctive reaction to aggressive emotions is to *lean forward*. That's why it's important to practice. (See #5 below.)

Even if you're not within reach, don't aim your strikes directly at the victim. When throwing a punch, aim straight past them, and never swing across their mid-line. Always use more distance than you think you need. I'd suggest aiming to miss by at least two feet.

If you can establish some kind of improvised weapon, do it. Swords, clubs, and even switchblades or broken bottles have length, which put you further away from your partner. And because you're striking with a space object, your hand won't come into contact. The act of looking for and grabbing a weapon also gives you an extra moment to slow down and think.

Weapons are powerful and intimidating. Bringing one out can give characters an option to stop a fight before it starts. Not actually fighting is the safest option.

3. *Slow-motion at all times*

ALWAYS deliver any violent action in slow-motion. It gives you more control over the movement, and your partner more time to see what's coming.

Slow-motion means slooooowwwww-moooootiooooon. Most people inaccurately judge their speed, and in performance the urge to make something happen causes us to speed up. A good guideline is that if it feels uncomfortable, it's probably slow enough. You might consider slowing down even more.

Even in slow-motion, don't actually touch the other person. You may want to show that moment of contact, with the squished face against the fist. But it's still easy to come in too fast, which will hurt. Always aim away from and move past the point of contact. Let your partner play the effect of taking the hit.

Avoid kicks. In slow-motion it's difficult to keep your balance, and you can pull a muscle or torque a knee joint.

4. *Telegraph your strikes*

Never lash out without warning. Your partner isn't a mind-reader, and you need to cue them even if the strike is coming slooooowwwwwly.

First, use a verbal cue. Think of 1930s movie comedies as an example—there's always some line of dialogue leading up to a punch. (*"I oughta sock you in the nose!" "Okay, that's it!" "Why, you . . .!"*) These signal that you're about to strike. Speaking a verbal cue is also a reminder to YOU to be careful.

Next, telegraph physically. A straight jab comes at you fast, even in slow-motion. A useful tip is to *lean away or take a step back first.* That creates more distance and gives the defender time to get ready. It's also another reminder to slow down.

Any punch or weapon attack should be much wider and bigger than normal. Think of those arcing ax swings in *The Lord of the Rings,* or the wild haymakers in *Rocky.* The bigger the motion, the better—using your large muscles gives you more control.

5. *Practice*

These are simple-enough concepts, but easily forgotten on stage. There are powerful forces of evolution at work here. Even with fake violence, your brain wants you to move forward and faster, which is a recipe for injury.

If you and your team decide to allow violence in your scenes, you need to get these skills into your muscle memory. Get together as often as you can to practice distance, slow-motion, and telegraphing.

Other Notes

Adding play to violence is a great way to add safety. For laughs, you can make it cartoonish, adding sound effects, crazy reactions, and milking those knockout moments. If you want to be serious, you can play up the realities of pain, blood, and physical exertion, as long as you're even more careful with your slow-motion.

Always discuss violent scenes in your post-show review. Were they done well? Did anyone get hurt? Did everyone feel safe? Use the learning opportunity to avoid future injuries.

Try the following exercises to practice improvised violence:

Trading Punches

Have players pair up and practice trading slow-motion punches, back and forth, using the techniques described in this chapter. Encourage them to move even more slowly than they think they should. *Players should never physically connect, even slowly.* Let the receiving player practice "taking" the punch, being careful not to strain.

After this has been well practiced, the receiving players can optionally try falling down—again in slow-motion (as described in the next section).

Poison-Arm Samurai

The group enacts a sword battle in slow-motion. Each player's outstretched arm is their "sword"—dipped in poison, one touch is lethal. Play everything in slow-motion—attacks, deaths, taunting opponents.

Watch for players speeding up to strike or avoid a touch. Discuss pursuing a personal agenda (surviving the game) at the cost of the reality of the scene (the slow-motion). Challenge players to risk getting caught, or allowing someone to get away, while remaining slow. Emphasize the importance of safety with stage violence.

Guns and Projectiles

If you choose to use a pistol, rifle, crossbow, blowgun, etc. in a scene, the safety issues are actually easier to deal with than hand-to-hand combat. The attacker doesn't do anything other than indicate a shot (maybe with help from the sound improviser). It's all in how the victim *receives* the bullet, which usually means some kind of falling down. That's the next topic.

Falls

Since the ancient discovery that banana peels are slippery, the prat-fall has been a go-to gag for physical comedians. There's something primally funny in seeing a person taken down by gravity.

But as anyone in orthopedic recovery will tell you, falling down hurts! And like staged violence, you need to do it carefully to avoid injury.

In 2001, The Second City Toronto staged *Family Circus Maximus*, directed by Michael Kennard of the world-famous clown duo Mump and Smoot. As an understudy for that show, I had to do one scene where a guy was visiting a therapist for crippling anxiety—he kept fainting, over and over.[2] Luckily, I got some rehearsal time with Mike, where he showed me how to fall down without significantly hurting myself.

Even with training, though, falling down is hard on the body. I only had to do that scene a few times a month and I got pretty bruised. I can't imagine what Paul Bates went through doing it nightly. I know he kept a pair of knee pads in the dressing room.

I tell this story because I want you to *seriously consider avoiding real-time falls*. It's always risky, and like I said before, you're not there to hurt yourself for anyone's amusement.

I won't explain what Mike taught me. I'm not fully trained, it's difficult to describe on paper, and I don't want you to be injured by doing it incorrectly. If it matters to you, take a workshop with an experienced acrobat or clown— it's great training for physical improv.[3] For everyone else, slow-motion is the way to go.

Fast or slow, the first principle for falls is *you MUST ALWAYS be aware of what's around you*. You don't want to hit a fellow player or a chair on the way down. Situational awareness is always important. (Go back and re-read that section earlier in this chapter.)

When falling in slow-motion, take as much time as you need to reach the floor. Watch your balance—if you lean over too far, gravity will catch you and you'll lose control. Keep a wide base in your legs, bend a knee, and place at least one hand on the ground before you "fall" the rest of the way. To repeat, *place* your hand—DO NOT FALL ON IT! Even from a height of inches, the jolt can cause a finger or wrist injury.

A safer alternative might be to slump into a nearby chair. Be sure your furniture is sturdy enough to handle it! Consider using slow-motion here too.

How this looks is all in the playing. If your character gets shot, you don't have to be blown away. You can react with surprise. You can look down at the wound. You can get a little wobbly. You can sit down, and then die. The only difference between comedy and drama might be how you say *"Arrrggghhh!"* as you go down. Either way, extending the moment with slow-motion is much safer.

---

[2] The therapist's comment was *"I can see how that might be difficult for an airline pilot."* After the 9/11 attacks in New York, this occupation was quickly changed to *"school bus driver."*
[3] *Combat Mime* contains instructions for various types of falls, written by an experienced fight choreographer. However, I still strongly recommend in-person training.

Audience Members

Safety importance doubles when you're involving audience members in the show. *You MUST protect your volunteers—often from themselves!*

People change when you put a spotlight on them. Some become bigger and louder, while others shrink and close up. In most cases, they're focused on trying to be funny, or not embarrassing themselves, or just getting through the scene. They're NOT paying attention to stage safety. You have to do this for them.

If you invite people on stage, make sure there's a safe way for them to get there. Always offer a hand and warn them to watch their step. If there aren't convenient and safe stairs, it may be better to have them stand at the foot of the stage.

Once volunteers are on stage, watch them closely. If they don't need to move in the scene, put them in chairs. If you need them walking, someone should stay close at all times. Players not in the scene might consider moving toward the edges of the stage, so they can jump in if someone is in danger of falling off.

Respect personal space. A short-form game like *Pillars*[4] may require you to touch the person on the shoulder as a signal. During your setup, ask them if it's okay to do this, and then demonstrate. Then do it *exactly the same way* in the scene—no surprises! Be ready to accommodate if anyone seems uncomfortable. Maybe you just point at them instead.

When the scene ends, volunteers are often in a hurry to leave the spotlight. Get near and keep them still until the lights are back up. It may require a hand on the shoulder and a polite word in their ear. When it's safe, help them step off the stage and return to their seats.

Regardless of the quality of the scene, *always* ask for a big round of applause for your volunteers. In formats with judging, if the scene gets a low score, ask for another score for the audience members, with judges always giving them top marks. Even if they weren't good, this encourages future volunteers.

Audience safety is deadly serious. The surest way to lose a crowd is to make people feel unsafe, embarrassed, or violated.

---

[4] A game where players occasionally pause during dialogue and get the volunteer to finish the line.

Promoting Physical Safety

Accidents are inevitable, but your team or company can minimize their frequency and severity by preparing in advance. Here are some ideas to build on.

Promote performer safety in rehearsals and classes. Teach exercises in slow-motion and telegraphing, and remind players to practice situational awareness at all times. Practice check-ins at the beginning and end of all events to report limitations and injuries. Post safety checklists in your studios and backstage.

Keep a well-stocked first aid kit ready for emergencies. If you own your own theatre space, also consider investing in an automated external defibrillator (AED)—these are lifesaving devices for both players and audience members. Make sure all directors and instructors know how to get to this equipment. It's also good to have a few staff trained in Emergency First Aid and CPR.

Finally, encourage your community to look out for one another to create fun but safe experiences. Let's all be careful out there!

15

Emotional Safety

Chapter Outline

Content Warning: This chapter discusses intimate physical contact between improv performers, including my own story of unwanted and uncomfortable touching. *If you're feeling distress as a result of similar experiences, please emphasize self-care as best you can.* There's a list of resources at the end of the chapter, and on the *Improv Illusionist* website (https://improvillusionist.com/emotional-safety).

Safety is not only for fighting and falling down. A humiliating or assaultive experience can be just as traumatic to the mind as violence is to the body, and maybe more. We can play *characters* who go through these experiences, but it's NOT okay if doing so will harm the *performer*. No actor should risk their mental health for the sake of entertainment.

Emotional Safety in the theatre is a very broad topic. Issues include stereotyping characters, cultural appropriation, power dynamics, micro-aggressions, harassment, and many others. Each is deeply nuanced, and there will always be debate over them. Nevertheless, we can all acknowledge that, intentionally or not, it's possible for one person's actions to hurt others. That awareness is the starting point. When every improviser understands the importance of safety, our art form will be more inclusive and enjoyable for everyone. It will also make it easier to spot and deal with the bad actors.

I understand that all of these issues are equally important. But given this book's focus on physical improv, I'm limiting the discussion here to *safety concerns when players make physical contact with each other*. People vary in their comfort with touch, lifting, and other interactions. Here we'll explore how to avoid situations that make players feel unsafe, and what can be done when they occur.

I acknowledge my cultural privilege as a white, straight, cisgender male. Even after many years of thinking about this, I know that I have blind spots and unconscious biases that may be reflected in my writing. Yet this conversation only advances if we have the courage to risk mistakes and learn from them. I welcome any and all feedback, and intend to update this chapter in future editions.

I'm indebted to the many beta readers who reviewed this material, most especially to Kaci Beeler of Austin, Texas. She is a founding member of the improv troupe *Parallelogramophonograph*, and teaches specialty workshops in Theatrical Intimacy, Stage Combat, and Consent. My conversation with Kaci informed the ideas in this chapter, but I take full responsibility for its content.

The Need for Physical Contact

It might seem the easiest thing to do is ban all physical contact. If there's no touching, there's no chance for people to feel uncomfortable or violated. For some improv groups, this may be a convenient and adequate solution.

That said, I don't believe it's workable for professional-level theatre. Improvisers must occasionally touch because human beings touch. We high-five and hug our friends. We embrace and kiss our lovers. Even strangers shake hands. Casual or intimate, comic or dramatic, physical connection expresses emotion and involvement in ways dialogue can never do. If theatre is a true reflection of our existence, we must include physical contact from time to time. Improvisers can *choose* to avoid all touching, but *insisting* on it creates cold, artificial characters and experiences.

Unfortunately, there are predators who take advantage of this, justifying atrocious behavior as *"what the scene called for."* Other players may be indifferent or willfully blind to balancing their need for attention with others' personal boundaries. These people will never acknowledge safety issues, and our improv community must stand against them.

The ideas in this chapter are meant for all well-meaning improvisers who want to create spectacular theatre without unintentional harm.

My Story

Most people don't think much about their boundary limits. You're among friends on a public stage—what's the worst that could happen? That was me in the early days of my improv career. I was *"up for anything,"* the wilder the better if it got a laugh. But you can never predict when or how your limits will be tested.

When I was first hired into The Second City Touring Company, I was thrilled. My skills and hard work had finally been recognized, and I was now part of the biggest theatre in improv. I also felt a low-lying anxiety. I knew that hundreds of other actors wanted to be where I was, and that the producers regularly reconsidered casting decisions. My position always felt precarious, especially at the beginning.

Not long after, I was filling in as an understudy for the Mainstage revue on a Saturday night. As the late show was ending, a group of improvisers from our community showed up in the greenroom. They asked if they could play in our post-show improv set. They had alcohol in hand, and it was clear they'd been drinking for a while. No one objected, though, and so they joined us.

Late-night Saturday sets are as unpredictable as improv gets. Booze has been flowing all evening, in the audience and sometimes backstage. The crowd is sometimes sleepy, sometimes fired up. And sometimes, performers decide to take them on. For our guests at least, this was one of those nights where the goal was to shock people.

In one scene, two of the guest actors were playing an important politician and their assistant. I stepped forward to fill in the stage picture, playing a security agent in the background. Suddenly, while continuing to talk to the assistant, the politician character began to casually grope me.

It was full hand-on-genitals, and it lingered. I didn't like it, and I definitely didn't consent to it. But the audience exploded with laughter. And here I was, on the biggest improv stage in Toronto, doing the job I'd wanted so badly. At that moment, as the silent, unmoving bodyguard, I felt the only way to do my job "well" was to let the scene play out. So I clenched my jaw and stood still while the groping continued.

I have since learned that this is a common reaction when we're confronted by an unsafe situation. When we feel unable to fight or flee, we instinctively freeze in an attempt to minimize injury. On the surface, no one saw anything unusual, and I later got much respect for my commitment to the scene. Inside, I was feeling intensely stressed and more than a little humiliated. And having chosen to play it out, I was marinating in those feelings.

This went on for nearly a full minute before someone edited the scene. I don't remember what else happened in that set, or how much I was able to play after that.

As we left the stage, the actor apologized. Wanting to look tough, I accepted the apology and left it at that. As far as I'm aware, this was an isolated event that happened in the context of that set. I've neither seen nor heard of this person doing anything similar in other shows. To this day, we're friendly colleagues.

Even so, there's no doubt that this was way beyond my boundary limit. Whether or not the actor intended to serve me up, it was a joke at my personal expense. And that's wrong.

This happened long before boundary conversations and reporting became recognized practices. I had no idea how to process the event. Given what I've learned about the long-term effects of the "stress-freeze" response, I've been lucky to avoid lasting trauma. But it definitely changed my view about being *"up for anything."*

The point of my story is that *Emotional Safety is an issue for ALL improvisers.* There's a common attitude that it's only about protecting women from predatory males. If that hasn't happened in a company, people minimize the issue. (*"That's not a problem for us."*) At least in terms of physical contact, safety concerns aren't limited to gender or power dynamics. *Anyone* can find themselves in an unsafe situation, even people like me, with all the privilege afforded by my male majority.

It's not just about intimate or sexual contact either. Stage violence, lifting, and similar actions can also cross boundaries. Improv is a team sport, and we must all be responsible for one another's safety.

Pressure

I believe most nonintentional safety issues arise from pressure to "succeed" with our improv. If you're new to performing, you may not have much experience with this. Reflecting on it away from the theatre helps everyone create safer performance and learning spaces.

Pressure is a constant force on every improviser at all levels of skill and performance. It could be pressure to get a reaction from a quiet audience; or to impress an important teacher, director, or agent; or to prove to ourselves that we're good improvisers. You can feel pressured in a show, a class, an audition, a rehearsal, or even just hanging out with your fellow actors. Others can put pressure on you, and you can put it on yourself.

This frequently shows up in the pressure to *accept ideas*. Collaboration and Yes–And are well-known concepts in improv, but they have a shadow side. We're trained not to kill scene ideas. We don't want people to judge our skills negatively, or label us as "difficult" to work with. So we may accept an offer or action even though it pushes our limits.

After an event that crosses a boundary, a common reaction is to feel guilt that we compromised ourselves. We ask how we could let that happen, why we didn't step back, redirect the offer, or kill the idea.[1] If we speak up about our concerns, others may ask those same questions, which can make us feel attacked and unsupported.

Choosing in the moment to "go along" does not make you any less human. Pressure can put us in impossible situations with no straightforward answers. For a while after my incident, I struggled with guilt over my choice and not talking about it afterward. Eventually, I found a way to give myself a break and let go of it. *If you're feeling distressed about an experience, please do whatever you can to look after yourself.* You can find many people out there who care and want to help.

Pressure shows up on the *initiating* side too. When a scene is dying, you may feel pressure to try something extreme to jolt it back to life. You can make dangerous choices even though you don't intend to harm anyone. A big reason why we learn slow-motion violence and techniques for lifting is to prevent injuries from improvisers lashing out under pressure to make

---

[1] "Don't kill ideas" is not a hard-and-fast rule in improv. Some ideas should be killed. Patti Stiles's book *Improvise Freely* has much more to say about this, and it should be required reading for every improviser.

something happen. Even so, equally dangerous actions like inappropriate touch or offensive dialogue can also show up.

The pressure to accept or initiate extreme ideas can be even stronger when you work at a higher level than you're used to. Examples might include being on stage with improvisers you admire, auditioning for a show, or playing scenes with your director or instructor. If you're an experienced player working with a rookie, remember that person may be feeling pressured by the situation. Be especially cautious about their safety.

As you grow in your improv career, you gain experience with pressure and get better at controlling your reaction to it. But those feelings never go away completely. The best we can do is watch for situations where pressure might be present and try to relieve it. If you spot something like this, make space for your fellow players as best you can. It might mean backing off on an offer, or editing a scene even if the audience is cheering it on. Watch especially for signs that a player is "frozen" by stress.

Playing to make your partner look good is a best practice that helps everybody. It's easier to notice and work with their reactions. And you will build scenes together, as opposed to one pressuring the other to go along.

Boundary Conversations

For some performers, a platonic hug or a casual hand on the shoulder is nothing. For others, it may be extremely uncomfortable. Depending on context, any type of touch can be felt differently from what's intended. In scripted theatre, we have hours of rehearsal to work out how actors can play safely. In improv, protecting players from harm is a unique problem.

A starting point is discussing boundaries away from the stage. Talk about how you feel when performing. Let people know your general comfort levels with physical contact. And take time for pre-show check-ins. Creating awareness makes everyone better able to work together.

Boundary conversations are easier and more efficient if you use a framework to structure them. This gives everyone a common language and procedures for communication. An excellent example comes from *Fair Play MN*, a collective of women/trans/femme/nonbinary comedians in Minnesota, USA.

The Fair Play framework defines four levels of increasing intimacy in touch and scene content. For example, a handshake is an example of "Level

A: Professional" touch, while intimate or violent contact is considered "Level D: Trusted." Once everyone understands what these levels mean, players can use them in pre-show check-ins to quickly express what they're comfortable with that day. (*"I'd prefer to stay within Level B."*) By consensus, groups can also set the level at which any class, rehearsal, or show will operate.

Fair Play also suggests a specific check-in practice after a show. Every player (so no one feels singled out) shares a point of celebration and a point of contention. Points of contention can include moments where players felt their boundaries were crossed, they didn't feel supported, or other ways for the group to improve.

As Fair Play says, the formality of these procedures is not to burden everyone. It's to remind people to tell others if their boundaries have changed, maybe because of a recent injury. Using a framework also helps normalize the conversation, so everyone gets comfortable talking about the issues.

And that's really the goal: to make these conversations a normal part of improviser safety. It's easy to walk the stage looking for physical hazards before a show. A quick boundary check-in is just as easy and just as important.

Whether you use them as published, or as a model for your own framework, I strongly recommend you visit the Fair Play MN website and download a copy of their resources. You'll find a link at the end of this chapter, and on the Emotional Safety page of the *Improv Illusionist* website (https://improvillusionist.com/emotional-safety).

Consent Practice

When improvising, reactions to pressure and the "stress-freeze" can be hard to notice. It's our job as actors to commit to a performance and hide ourselves—and we get very good at it. You can play for a long time with someone and never know they're in distress. And it's not like we have our boundary limits printed on our foreheads.

The easiest way to protect your partner is to *ask for and receive clear consent* before getting physical. There's nothing wrong with asking *"Can I touch you?"* and getting a clear "yes"/"no" answer. Same with *"Want a hug?"* or *"Can I pick you up?"* or *"Is it okay if I . . .?"* And there's nothing wrong with replying *"No"* either.

Many people think about consent only in its sexual context. On stage, it applies to *any* interaction where you contact another person, especially lifts.

When you've had a *clear boundary check-in* prior to the performance, you may not have to do this for certain "benign" contact, like touching the shoulder, holding hands, or adjusting someone's clothing (as long as they're within that person's expressed boundary). Still, asking for consent is always available, and if in doubt you should always err on the side of doing it.

Yes, you CAN do this in any scene! There are many ways to ask for consent, including character dialogue or a quick *sotto voce* confirmation between improvisers. Like any other skill, it might seem awkward at first. Or you may worry that somehow your scenes will break by taking a beat to confirm consent. (They won't.)

It just takes practice. Kaci Beeler has kindly allowed me to share the following exercises she uses in her workshops.

Consent Practice Exercises by Kaci Beeler

1. *Practice saying "No"*

In this exercise, performers and students are asked to practice saying "no" within a simple script:

Person A: "Can I touch your elbow?"
Person B: "No, you may not."
Person A: "Thank you, for telling me!"
Person B: "Thank you, for asking!"

Then repeat with Person B asking Person A if they can do something with them/to them. It doesn't always have to be touching-related; it can be, *"Can I say something crude to you?"* or *"Can I wiggle my eyebrows at you?"*—but the answer will always be, *"No, you may not,"* or *"No, you cannot."* Some participants may want to say, *"No, not right now, maybe later!"* But it's important to practice giving a firm "no" and also important to follow it up with the two "thank you" sentences at the end.

Once this has been done a few times (and maybe switching partners a few times as well), try the second version below.

2. *Practice setting boundaries*

In this version, which is best preceded by the *Practice Saying "No"* exercise, performers and students are given a situation where they ask their partners for permission to touch them or do something to or with them. The simple script is back:

Person A: "Can I touch your elbow?"
(Person B can take a moment to think if they are truly okay with this or not, and then answer truthfully if possible.)
Person B: "Yes, you may touch my elbow!" (presents elbow)
(Person A touches elbow.)
Person A: "Thank you, for telling me I could do that!"
Person B: "Thank you, for asking!"

Or the result could look the same as the script example in the "No" Exercise:

Person A: "Can I touch your face?"
Person B: "No, you may not."
Person A: "Thank you, for telling me!"
Person B: "Thank you, for asking!"

Or the result can have a redirect:

Person A: "Can I touch your face?"
Person B: "No, you cannot touch my face but you can touch my shoulder."
Person A: "Okay, I am comfortable with that!"
(Person B presents shoulder, Person A touches shoulder and removes hand.)
Person A: "Thank you, for telling me what you are okay with."
Person B: "Thank you, for asking!"

If someone answers with hesitation like, *"Hmmm . . . I think you can touch my face?"* the answer is actually a "NO." **Only an Enthusiastic YES is a Yes.** This response should be celebrated as well by both parties and a redirect that is perhaps less invasive could be suggested.

Person A: "Can I touch your elbow?"
Person B: ". . .Yes? I think so?"
Person A: "That sounds like a 'no.' How about your hand?"
Person B: "Yes! You can touch my hand!"

A person can even decide to say "NO" after they've already said "YES" and that's okay too!

Person A: "Can I touch your elbow?"
Person B: "Yes, you may!"
(Person A reaches toward Person B)

Person B: "Wait! I'm not comfortable with that!"
Person A: "No problem! Thank you, for telling me!"
Person B: "Thank you, for understanding. Can we high-five instead?"
Person A: "Yes! I would love to high-five!"
(The two people high-five each other)

These exercises may seem simple, but even as children many of us weren't taught to ask for permission, give boundaries, or express gratitude for learning about and setting boundaries with others. It's not too late to practice, and you might be surprised by what you learn about yourself and your boundaries. Remember—boundaries are not static—they are constantly changing! If we celebrate our boundaries, it's not as painful to set them or respect them.

As Kaci says, please don't dismiss these exercises because they seem easy or awkward. To normalize the process of sharing consent, it's important to say these words and to hear them. This is no different from the way we encourage beginning improvisers to literally say *"Yes, and . . ."* to each other's offers.

Deliberately practicing consent this way trains you to think about it in performance. With experience and skill, you can find ways to ask for and receive consent that seem more natural. Even if you can only think to do it this way in a scene, do it. Not only does it keep everyone safe, there's a sweetness in respecting consent that can actually make your characters more likable.

NEVER ASSUME CONSENT—EVER. And be aware that a person's consent can change, anytime, for any reason. If you're unsure that you have clear consent, or if you become unsure any time after receiving consent, listen to those instincts. You MUST change your action, no matter what's happening in the scene. Adapting to the needs of all players is everyone's responsibility.

Even with consent, the safest approach is to *avoid directly putting your hands on someone.* Instead, let them come to you. Make good eye contact, stop short of touching, and give the player the chance to accept or move away. For example, you can hold out your arms for a hug and let them come to you. Or not. Let it be their choice.

And remember that the option to *avoid* physical contact is always there. If you're not 100 percent certain about consent, DON'T touch!

Consent versus Yes–And

Please remember that consent is *a clear, affirmative expression* of an actor's agreement to physical contact. That may sound the same as saying *"Yes, and . . ."* to an offer, but it's not. *Consent and Yes–And are VERY different.*

Especially among beginning improvisers, Yes–And is often misunderstood as *"you must accept any offer you are given."* Some players exploit this to justify offers that make themselves look good at the expense of others.

Saying "Yes" to an offer does not mean simply going along with everything your partner wants. Players can and do say "No" to each other without killing the idea between them. It just means you explore that idea differently. Any improviser who insists you have to take an offer a specific way (their way) is not a team player.[2]

To be absolutely clear, Yes–And is NOT a justification for:

- manipulating scene partners into uncomfortable situations, intentionally or not;
- accusing players of blocking when they redirect or resist an offer;
- harassing actors because they didn't *"just go along"* with an action and/ or *"made a big deal"* about it later; or
- risking anyone's physical or mental health (including your own) for the sake of a show, class, or potential job.

These are all ways of pressuring actors into dangerous situations.

Consent beats Yes–And every time.

Kaci pointed out to me that there can be *two different types of "Yes"*—the character's and the actor's—and that they can be different. For example, a character can say "Yes" to a sexual advance even if the actor doesn't consent to touching. Playing that scene takes some creativity and is actually a fun challenge. How could you play characters having sex without physically touching each other?

When You Feel Unsafe

It's your right to refuse any physical interaction that crosses your personal boundaries or makes you feel uncomfortable. It's important to remember

---

[2] Again, I recommend Patti Stiles's book *Improvise Freely* for more about these important issues.

this, because players, teachers, or directors watching your scene may not see or understand your discomfort. Waiting for someone to intervene leaves you open to the possibility that they won't.

To be clear, you do NOT have to confront anyone or take responsibility for correcting them, especially if it makes you feel even more unsafe. What I'm saying is that you can always take action to protect yourself.

On stage, pressure can make this challenging. One way to do it is to let your personal reaction fuel the actions of your character. For example, if you're playing lovers but don't want to kiss your scene partner, you can refuse the kiss in character. There are plenty of reasons why a lover might refuse a kiss. Maybe they want to have a serious talk, or maybe they're angry that the laundry wasn't finished. Redirecting an offer like this is completely possible without breaking a scene.

Sometimes, if a partner isn't being safe, and they're not getting the message from how you're playing, breaking character may be the only way to get through to them. Make clear eye contact and tell them to stop. I've seen some actors try to conceal this under their breath, turning their back to the audience or waiting for a laugh to cover it. Don't worry about that—make your message clear.

If you work regularly with the same group, you can all agree in advance on a safety gesture. I know some players who drop to one knee and cross their arms to signal they need a time-out.

And *you can always leave or end a scene anytime*, even if you have to call an edit yourself.

All of this equally applies in workshops and rehearsals. Be aware that it's part of a teacher's job to gently push students out of their comfort zone. Your instructor may choose not to side-coach or stop a scene, preferring to talk about any issues afterward. Even so, they should always respect your right to withdraw from an uncomfortable situation anytime.

Reporting Unsafe Events

By *reporting*, I mean speaking up to one or more people about an experience of feeling unsafe. This could be a formal report filed with your theatre company, but it could also be as simple as saying, *"I didn't feel safe when you picked me up in that lumberjack scene."*

If a boundary issue comes up in a show, class, or rehearsal, try to report it in notes afterward. Others may not have noticed there was a problem, and the discussion helps everyone learn.

However, be aware that sometimes people don't process their reaction to events immediately. Your feelings about an incident may change, and you have the right to report a safety issue *anytime*. It's no less valid or important just because you *"didn't speak up at the time."*

You don't have to report issues involving a specific person to that person. Your company or training facility should have one or more designated people to accept reports and investigate.

If you don't feel safe reporting to *anyone,* that's okay too. It may help to find friends who can support you or speak on your behalf. Also consider reporting anonymously, so issues are at least raised without you feeling exposed or harassed. Theatre companies should have a policy and communication channels for this.

If there are continuing or systemic problems in your company, you may have to decide whether you want to keep reporting multiple events. Changing a toxic environment isn't easy. If your concerns continue to go unaddressed, you may have to consider finding a different, more supportive group to play with. That outcome is sad and unfair, but you must prioritize your own safety. Once you're in a better environment, you may be able to call for change from outside your former group. An internet search can help you find support and other resources for performers.

Above all, look after yourself. Find someone you can share your experience with, so you don't have to keep it inside. This may be a fellow improviser, but consider that someone outside the community may be able to support you with a different perspective.

Promoting Emotional Safety

Because of its spontaneity, we can never guarantee a completely "safe space" for improv. But everyone in our community has a role in making our performing and learning spaces *SAFER*. Here are a few suggestions to build on.

Performers

Remember that Emotional Safety is an issue for *everyone*. It's no less important than preventing physical injury. Practice asking for, giving, and withholding consent. Talk about boundaries and do pre- and post-show check-ins. Watch for stage pressure and stress-freezes and be ready to react.

Respect everyone's right to redirect or reject an uncomfortable offer. Play to make your partner look good.

Listen when others talk about Emotional Safety. If these are new issues for you, it can be easy to become defensive. Stay present and listen to the person speak. Take their side and acknowledge events from their point of view. Then talk about how you can adjust for future situations. Use the same great communication skills you practice in your improv.

As Kaci Beeler suggests, make it a habit to *always say "Thank you"* for a person's courage to raise an issue. Even if the conversation is contentious, we need to establish that it's okay to speak up.

Directors and Instructors

Recognize your role as an influencer in your community. Teach, model, and draw attention to performer safety. Practice consent and boundary check-ins in classes and rehearsals. Watch for pressure situations and be prepared to side-coach or end a scene. In discussion, avoid singling out players—talk about how the group can do better.

Allow space for performers to flag safety issues after a show, audition, or workshop. You may not want a detailed discussion to distract from your notes, but you can always make room for it afterwards. It's tremendously empowering for performers to be able to say, *"I felt unsafe when . . ."* and feel truly heard by a mentor.

Because of your position and experience, be aware that your mere presence can be intimidating. It may pressure others to act unpredictably or go along in silence. *Be especially cautious when you play scenes with your cast or students.* Recognize that there is a power imbalance in these situations.

Be transparent with your directing or teaching objectives, and be open to different ways of achieving them. Reports of unsafe experiences or boundary concerns are ABSOLUTELY NO REASON for recasting, reprisals, or devaluing a performer. You must at least *consider* changing your approach. Create reporting safety by appointing an assistant director or other unbiased person who can discuss issues.

Theatre Companies and Training Centers

Protect the physical and mental health of your members. Create policies and procedures for performer/student safety, anti-harassment, and nondiscrimination. Appoint dedicated persons responsible for taking and investigating reports. Provide anonymous reporting options. This is a *necessary* part of your work.

Develop a Code of Conduct and have everyone regularly agree to abide by it. This sets expectations for shows, rehearsals, and classes, and makes it easier to deal with problematic people. Commit your directors and instructors to education on these issues and encourage them to model safety.

Seek equity, diversity, and inclusion in your casting and show offerings. Diversity contributes to increased Emotional Safety. It's also just the right thing to do. Improv is a team sport, and everyone should be allowed to play, safely and respectfully.

Offer workshops in Physical and Emotional Safety and encourage all players to attend. Review the content of your classes and look for ways to diversify your training.

Working Through Fear and Uncertainty

Taking action to address Emotional Safety will likely feel awkward and uncomfortable at first. There may be push-back from some members of your community. There may be a dip in show quality or audience interest. You may face pressure to slow down or even reverse your plans. Some people may leave.

This is all part of the process of normalizing new ideas. If players have never practiced boundary check-ins or asking for consent, reordering their thinking may affect their improv for a while. Diverse and inclusive shows may struggle at first, simply because the players haven't been given prior opportunities to work together. Audiences like what's familiar and have trouble adjusting to new offerings.

As new practices become normalized, however, you will create a community where everyone feels comfortable to play at their highest level. When that happens, the quality of your shows and workshops will flourish.

Improvisation is all about embracing fear, uncertainty, and the possibility of failure. We counter these with courage, commitment, and patience. If we want to live up to the promise of our art form, we need to do this together. It's all about looking after our partners.

Resources for Emotional Safety Issues

Visit https://improvillusionist.com/emotional-safety for an updated and expanded version of this list. Please help our community by sending me links to any helpful information you find.

NOTE: I'm based in Canada and have the most familiarity with resources for North America. To find resources local to you, try an online search using keywords from the titles of these resources.

Sexual Misconduct Resources

- For local help, try the following online search: *sexual assault help [city] [country]*.
- (USA) National Sexual Assault Hotline: 1-800-656-HOPE (4673).
- (USA) RAINN (Rape, Abuse & Incest National Network): https://www .rainn.org/
- (Canada) Kids Help Phone: 1-800-668-6868.
- (Canada) see "Harassment Resources" link below.
- "Resources on Sexual Abuse and Misconduct in Theatre." *Theatre Communications Group.* https://www.tcg.org/Default.aspx?TabID =6697

Boundary Check-Ins and Levels of Intimacy

- "Boundaries Conversation Guidelines Brochure." *Fair Play MN.* https://fairplaymn.wordpress.com/documents/

Developing Anti-Harassment Policies

- "Preventing Harassment and Discrimination in Your Improv Theater." *The Improv Network.* http://www.theimprovnetwork.org/harassment -in-your-improv-theater/
- "Harassment Resources." *Artist Producer Resource.* https://artistprodu cerresource.ca/tiki-index.php?page=Harassment (includes links and information for Canadian crisis resources)

Example Theatre Policies and Codes of Conduct

- "Anti-Harassment & Non-Discrimination Policy." *Bad Dog Theatre Company.* https://baddogtheatre.com/anti-harassment-and-non-discrimination-policy
- "Code of Conduct." *The Hideout Theatre.* https://www.hideouttheatre.com/code-of-conduct
- "Student Handbook & Safety Contract." *Improv Cincinnati.* https://improvcincinnati.com/student-info
- "Code of Behaviour." *Royal Court Theatre.* https://royalcourttheatre.com/code-of-behaviour
- "Public Theater Code of Conduct." *The Public Theater.* https://publictheater.org/about/code-of-conduct2

Further Reading on Improv and Consent

- "Improv & Consent: Why 'Yes, And' doesn't always mean Yes." *Hayley Kellett (The Making Box).* https://www.themakingbox.ca/blog/2018/4/17/improv-consent-why-yes-and-doesnt-always-mean-yes
- "Intimacy and Boundaries in Improv." *Neil Curran (Lower the Tone).* https://www.lowerthetone.com/2018/03/intimacy-and-boundaries-in-improv/
- "'C' is for 'Consent.'" *David Charles (Improv Doctor).* https://improvdr.com/2021/05/03/c-is-for-consent/

Part VI

The Working Improviser

To close out the book, I want to share some "bonus" notes from my career experience as an improv performer and teacher. If you're a beginning improviser, or looking to make the leap from amateur to professional, these ideas may help as you develop your own approach to the work.

You Will Learn

- how to prepare for and get the most out of your improv shows;
- tips for performing improv online—and especially how to be more physical inside the camera frame; and
- ideas for instructors teaching physical improv.

16

Performing and Learning from Shows

It may seem strange to talk about preparing for an improv show. How do you prepare for spontaneous events to happen? Why prepare at all?

Well, the content may be improvised, but there's a lot of structure in every show. Unless you open cold on a single monoscene, you'll need a host to welcome the audience and explain what's going on. If you're doing short-form games, you'll decide what to play and what suggestions to ask for. These structures are predictable, and you should have a plan for how they'll unfold.

Overconfidence is a real danger for improv shows. It's common for players to show up late to the venue and do the bare minimum to prepare. Everyone thinks they can wing it through any problems. Then something goes awry, and the unprepared response makes the show seem amateurish.

I've been guilty of this too. On most show nights, I'm usually feeling a touch of anxiety. Talking through the details feels like I'm spending too much time in my head. When asked what I'd like to do, I'd rather say *"Whatever"* and go with the flow.

As always, we have to think about the audience. If you're asking people to give up their time and money to come to your show, they deserve a quality experience. It doesn't matter if you're in a church basement or a prime 300-seat theatre. They notice if you're stammering through your setups because you need a different game and can't think of one. They notice if your scenes are similar to earlier acts in the show. They notice if you haven't prepared.

What I've learned is that a show always goes more smoothly when you plan its structure. By thinking about ideas before you get to the theatre, it's easier for everyone to build a show with more variety. And by knowing what comes next, you can feel comfortable to take the brakes off your improv and just play.

Another reason to think about your shows in advance is that it's a fast route to becoming a better performer. Every show is a learning opportunity, but you can never guarantee what experience you'll get. Good preparation helps you get the most benefit from your stage time.

You will eventually develop your own preparation process, but if you're looking for ideas, the following have worked well for me over the years.

Tools

Get a *notebook* and bring it everywhere—shows, workshops, rehearsals, planning meetings. A hardback, spiral-bound notebook works really well. It's got a built-in writing surface. It lies flat so you can easily look at it while you're working (for set lists, suggestion prompts, etc.). You can tear pages out if your team needs spare paper. And the spiral is a perfect place to store a pen.

Your notebook helps you track patterns. Your memory is terrible for doing this. By recording sets and notes, and your thoughts about them, you'll see both good and bad patterns emerge. Below, I'll talk about the kind of notes you could make.

A *water bottle* is also good to have. Improv can be very athletic. If you're sweating or feeling dry, some hydration between scenes can keep you going. Drinking water also forces you to breathe, which can calm stage anxiety.

Consider also the *clothing* you're wearing for shows and workshops. Flip back to page 124 for more about this.

Carry a *small bag or backpack* for storing your stuff while at the venue. It's safest to empty your pockets before a show, and you never know what the security will be like. A single bag is easy to hand to your stage manager. Consider a small luggage padlock to hold the zippers closed if you're worried about your wallet or phone.

Before the Show

Look through your notebook for thoughts from previous shows. Identify skills you want to work on or negative patterns you want to avoid. Use these to create one or two *objectives* for the upcoming show. I don't recommend more than two. Too many objectives may push you to steamroll scenes and not work with your ensemble. Plan for moments where you might work deliberate skills.

Try to make your objectives specific. *"Be more physical"* is okay, but it doesn't give you anything to latch onto. It's better to have a more detailed goal, like *"do one scene where I play around with object work."* Or *"do an outdoors scene and try to hit all five senses."*

If your objective is to avoid a negative pattern—such as *"avoid asking so many questions"*—try to have a positive goal to go with it. Even better, try to frame negative goals as positive: *"Make more assumptions."*

Along with objectives, make a list of previous characters or scene premises to bring back and explore. Refreshing your memory on these will make them easier to call to mind during the show.

For short-form, know your games and how to set them up! Practice introducing them and getting suggestions quickly. A clean, quick setup keeps the show moving.

If you know in advance who you'll be playing with, you could have your pre-show check-in by chat or phone before you even get to the venue. Then you can relax and keep your head clear backstage.

Before you head out for the show, take some time to stretch. Depending on what's happening at the venue, you may not get much time to do it there. It's also a good way to leave other things behind and transition to your performer's head space.

At the Venue

Respect your call time. Your stage manager may need help setting up or have special instructions for you. Arrive early if you can.

When you get to the venue, your first priority should be *safety*. Walk the stage and look for physical dangers. Check in with your fellow players and see how they're feeling. Ask about any physical limitations, boundaries, or other issues. (Go back to the chapters on Physical and Emotional Safety for considerations.)

Then, build your set list. If you're doing short-form, everyone should suggest one game to play. Be definitive, not wishy-washy. Challenge yourself—don't pick the same games all the time. Also think about what suggestions you want to get for each scene and creative ways to ask for them.

If you're playing a game format like Theatresports, you'll also have to think of challenges for each round. The temptation here is to fit the challenge to the games you've chosen. For example, to justify games like *A-to-Z* or *Number of Words*, you might challenge the other team to *"a word-restriction scene"* or *"a scene involving language."* But these tip the audience off to what you're about to do. They also lock you into particular types of games, which is a problem for variety, especially if an earlier group played similar games. Make your challenges open-ended, like *"a scene about crime"* or *"best scene featuring an animal."*

Chat with other groups on the same bill and make adjustments for variety. We always want the audience seeing different things. Keep a couple of backup ideas in mind in case you need to change up your set on the fly.

Write out your set list in someone's notebook (or more than one). Note down who will introduce each segment and what they will ask for. Bring it with you on stage. Keep your water bottle handy, but be careful it doesn't become an obstacle on the stage.

During the Show

Even if you're only performing in one segment, watch the whole show! Not only is this respectful to the other performers, you will know what the audience has already seen. Avoid repeating locations, relationships, topics, and suggestion questions, even between different parts of the show. Variety is the improviser's best friend because it never gives the audience a straight comparison between scenes or players. You need to be constantly ready to adjust your set.

On stage, think about your show objectives, but *hold them loosely*. If you don't get a chance to meet them, that's okay! Keeping goals in mind trains you to look for opportunities, and it's this instinct you want to build. Steamrolling a show for your personal goals is not cool.

It's a safe practice to clear the stage of furniture and objects between every scene. This is also a visual cue that you're resetting the stage picture.

Help each other out with the presentation. When a scene ends, the nearest player to the written running order can check it and signal to the next presenter. Teamwork isn't just for your scenes.

When you're in the backline or on a team that's not currently playing, *look interested*. The audience can see you.

And of course, PLAY and HAVE FUN!

After the Show

Know your group's post-show procedure. Some give everyone five minutes to gather their things and say a quick hello to friends and family, while others do notes right away. Don't keep your fellow players waiting—everyone wants to get out of there.

Director's notes are meant to make both the show and the improvisers better. Take them in that spirit, especially the negative ones. It sucks to feel called out in front of a group. We've all been there. Sometimes you just have to say *"thank you,"* and move on. If you want to defend yourself or ask for more feedback, you can discuss it later after notes.

The exceptions to this are *issues of safety and respect*. We all need to work together to create communities where players feel safe, and can speak their mind about situations where they didn't feel that way. These issues need to be mentioned in the group to increase awareness and help prevent similar situations. Some directors don't like interruptions to their notes—ask for permission to flag an issue and then take it to discussion later.

It's a quirk of professional etiquette that actors avoid giving direct notes to each other. At the very least, you should ask permission, but it's often better to avoid it. Instead, try to use I-statements to avoid ascribing motives to other players, such as, *"I felt unsafe in that jungle office scene."* Or try to offer group solutions for the future: *"Can we practice lifting or talk about ways to do it more safely?"*

If someone flags something you did, try not to take it personally or leap to defend yourself. Listen and thank them for speaking up. Work together constructively, the same way you do on stage.

Don't close the books on a show without writing a few notes to yourself. Some things to note, if they came up in the show:

- scenes that went especially well or poorly;
- audience reactions (positive and negative) to specific moments;
- interesting characters or premises you could explore again;
- good lines of dialogue (whether in the scene or thought of afterward like all improvisers do);
- games that worked or didn't work;
- skills you did well or want to improve;
- goals you met or didn't meet;
- notes from the post-show meeting; and
- personal feelings about the show.

Include enough detail that you can make sense of it later. Improv is so ephemeral you might barely remember a show you did last week. Yes, it's a hassle to do this when you'd rather hit the bar or go home to sleep. A few minutes' work while your memory is fresh will pay off when you're preparing for the next show or workshop.

When making notes, try to balance positives and negatives. Most people tend to bias themselves one way or the other, usually toward the negative. Even a terrible show has moments of good work. Be proud of your achievements and take note of your strengths.

Check yourself for injuries. Adrenaline is weird—you can bump into objects or pull muscles and not feel it until much later. If you've had an especially physical show, some extra stretching is a good idea before you go to bed. Be careful of any muscles you may have strained during the show. And if you discover any injuries that are due to a safety concern, be sure to bring them up to your producer.

Finally, *celebrate!* Large or small, good or bad, you contributed to our crazy, wonderful art-form. It's a courageous act—reward yourself for it.

Break a leg on your next show!

17

Improvising Online

In recent years, Zoom and other broadcasting solutions have created fantastic new opportunities for improv learning and performance. Players worldwide can now meet up and jam anytime. Instructors have expanded their class offerings by teaching online. And many companies are expanding on the technology. At the time of writing this book, there have been at least two online platforms built specifically for improv, and even a few experiments with shows in virtual reality. Whatever form it eventually takes, it's safe to say online improv is here to stay.

From my own performing and teaching experience, here are some tips that can make improvising online easier and more effective. And for the improv illusionist, I'll include ideas for adding environment and physicality to your online scenes.

Understanding the Differences

You might think that film and TV actors would have an advantage when improvising over a video stream. They don't—improv on Zoom is much different from simple camera work.

The biggest problem is *eye contact*. To play "out" to the audience, you need to look into the camera lens. This takes your eyes off the screen, so you can't really watch and react to a scene partner. The lack of visual cues leads to a lot of overtalk, so it's even more important to *slow down and listen.*

The other major difference is *audience response*. The audience is an essential partner in all theatre, and when performing online we drastically feel the loss of their contribution. You can try leaving microphones open for laughter, or encouraging live reactions in chat, but these are nowhere near the same. Many improvisers have resisted or abandoned online improv for this reason.

For me, losing audience response has actually been helpful for re-evaluating why I improvise. At first, I was sad about performing online—it felt too quiet and isolating. I realized just how much I'd needed the external validation from an audience. I decided to focus instead on returning to the basics of shared storytelling—listening, heightening offers, valuing and entertaining my partner. When I started *playing* more, I felt more enjoyment. I still want the audience back, but finding internal validation from play has been my key to success online.

General Tips for Online Improv

It's hard to attract (and keep) audiences online, so you should do everything possible to maximize the quality of your show experience. These tips will help.

Equipment

Assuming your computer has a built-in microphone and webcam, you can start immediately. Still, you will likely get better results by upgrading your equipment. If your budget is limited, prioritize your microphone. Audiences can cope with suboptimal video, but poor audio chases them away. Also consider wearing a set of earbuds to prevent microphone echo from your speakers. You can find clear-colored earbuds online that are far more unobtrusive than those bright white AirPods. Wear them behind your head to hide the cable.

Good lighting is also helpful. Natural light from a window is great if available, but point the camera *away* from the light so it doesn't wash out the video. Clip-on ring lights are cheap, and can fit right over a laptop's camera lens. Or, you can just as easily use a couple of lamps, placed at eye-level on either side of your setup to minimize shadows. Avoid overhead lighting unless you have at least one other light source for balance.

I talk about backdrops in the next part of this chapter. However, they're not necessary if you can set up in front of a neutral wall.

Prepare in Advance

Wrangle your technology to get the best video and audio performance. Connect to the call early and test your connection strength. If possible, use a wired internet connection instead of wi-fi. Pause or shut down any unnecessary apps on your device so they don't hog extra bandwidth. This includes sync apps (like Dropbox or OneDrive) and websites that continuously update themselves (like Gmail or Facebook).

If you're sharing anything on your screen as part of the show, have the files open and ready. Know how to share a single window versus your whole screen, and practice so you can do it quickly.

At Oakville Improv, we've experimented with sharing video for voice-dubbing scenes, but it's tricky due to potential lag. Everyone's connection must be rock solid. If the improviser can't see the video running smoothly, they can't keep up. If you try it, avoid streaming video from YouTube or elsewhere. Download the video to your local device and play it from there.

Use a Producer (More Than One)

The video meeting's host controls all aspects of the broadcast, including muting audience members. Players in your show can do this, but it's easier to have a dedicated producer at the helm. Ideally, you could have more than one person doing this, focusing on different jobs like screen sharing, monitoring the audience, and moderating the chat.

Set Yourself up for Success

Explore ALL the settings in your video-meeting software. "Advanced" settings can sometimes compensate for audio or lighting, but I recommend you avoid tinkering with these unless you have a real performance problem. Experiment, and then reset everything back to defaults before setting up the options that work.

Learn the keyboard shortcuts for various functions. At minimum, you should know how to quickly turn your camera and microphone on/off for entrances/exits. Some apps like Zoom have configurable shortcuts. You can change these to make keystrokes easier, and turn some shortcuts off completely to avoid "fat fingers" accidents (especially the shortcut to *End Meeting*).

Most software "mirrors" your video back to you, so you see yourself as you're used to in the mirror. Consider turning this option off so you can see exactly what the audience sees. If it's important for you to point to the left or right, you'll want to know how it looks to observers.

Set the Audience up for Success

Many companies broadcast shows to YouTube or Twitch to avoid audience interaction issues. However, if you're inviting people to join your online meeting, prepare setup instructions for them to get the best experience. Send these in advance with the meeting invitation. You could make a dedicated page on your website, including screenshots for how to set up the various options. This takes a bit of work but is completely worth it.

Tell your audience to arrive a few minutes early so you can go over the setup instructions with them. Use the Waiting Room function to keep latecomers from accidentally popping up in the middle of a scene. You may decide to let people in when there's a suitable break in the show.

Use Gallery View

Most of the time, everyone (audience and players) should use Gallery View. This keeps the video from jumping around every time someone makes a noise. Hide nonvideo participants to make the individual screens bigger. Only performers in a scene should have their camera on.

Remember that Gallery View doesn't present in the same order on everyone's screen. If your scene partner's video frame is on your left, you can't reliably "turn" to face them and expect everyone to see the same thing.

Environment and Physicality for Online Improv

The mostly fixed format of a video call is quite limiting, especially for someone like me who's used to more physicality. For the most part, you have to keep your head and shoulders visible so you can be seen in a Gallery View with a large group. Still, there are a few ways to put more environment and movement into online improv.

Be Affected by Your Environment

This is the biggest one, anytime. Environment can affect your character's attitude, emotions, and reactions. On video, you'll need to be more specific about how it's doing so.

Consider temperature, sounds, smells, and anything else that might affect you in the place you're in. What might you see in the environment? What's going on around you? (Reviewing this book's Part III on Environment will help, especially the notes on outdoor environments and "What's Beyond?")

Get More Space

Not everyone has the space to move around. But it's ideal if you have room to step back from the camera and move with your whole body. Even if you're trapped at a desk in a tiny office, you might be able to make some space for spinning in your chair, or moving out of frame.

Use Props

Unfortunately, object work doesn't seem to translate very well to online improv. We're all too conditioned from watching film and TV with realistic objects. Gather props, hats, glasses, and other accessories close by. You can switch up what you're wearing to show environment, such as wearing a jacket if it's cold.

For some neat visuals, match props with your partners. This gives you the option to "give" something into the camera, and your partner "receives" it out the other end. For example, one character can hand a tissue to a crying friend.

Keep Your Object Work Clear

Despite the above, you can still handle space objects if it becomes necessary to the scene. Specifics are even more important to help people read what you're doing. Make sure your hands are out front and visible in the frame. Take your time and exaggerate your movements slightly.

Use the Frame

Being on camera doesn't mean you have to *stay* on camera. If you're able to stand up, you can exit and enter from different sides of the frame. In a swimming scene, for example, you can pop up from the water by jumping up from below.

Try to match your body framing (head and shoulders, full body, etc.) with the other players. If you all look the same size, it's easier to believe you're inhabiting the same space.

Change Camera Angles

Experiment with your webcam settings. I found that on Zoom, you can adjust the rotation of the video output. One thing I tried was upside down. By putting my arms up over my head, and swaying side to side, it looked like I was hanging from the ceiling by my ankles. You can physically turn the camera on its side, too. These are limited use situations, but something to play with.

Move the Device

Using a smartphone or tablet will give you more freedom to move around. You could stage different backdrops around your room for environment changes. I've also seen fun long-form shows where players broadcast from unusual locations, like outside or in the bathtub.

Be aware that certain app features may be missing or limited on mobile, such as Chat or Gallery View. All players will need a backup plan in case someone's mobile connection degrades.

If you move around while on camera, be careful about distracting from others or causing vertigo in the audience!

Try Cinematic Tricks

The camera gives you many options for creative shots. In one scene, my friend James Jeffers "embraced" another character, then spun in place so the background behind him whipped around. It looked like the classic "hug and turn" shots we see in romance movies. Funny stuff.

If you're using a wireless device, you could also try panning or tracking shots. These are even better if you have an extra person available to hold and move the camera.

Mind Your Background

Watching people perform from their home office or living room quickly shows you the value of a theater's blank stage. The sight of bookshelves or furniture in the background undermines any sense of environment you might be trying to create. Use a neutral, distraction-free background (like a bare wall) whenever possible. If all players use a similar background, it's easier to believe they're in the same space.

If you have the budget, consider a photography background kit. They're relatively inexpensive, and include the rigging to hang a drape behind you. Some kits are also bundled with lights, but think carefully about the expense. How much use do you expect to get out of this equipment? A cheaper option might be to mount a clothesline and hang a neutral-colored bedsheet.

Virtual backgrounds are fun to tinker with. You can upload your own images if you want a specific environment. At Oakville Improv, we've used multiple images of the same place but with slightly different angles, so everyone can be in a shared location without it looking exactly the same. For virtual backgrounds to be most effective, though, you really need to use a proper green screen. Zoom's "adaptive view" gets easily confused by a lot of movement, and its flickering is very distracting. Use lots of light on your green screen—shadows can also cause flickering.

Above all, feel free to experiment and keep innovating! Online improvisation is still in its infancy. It's exciting to see the new experiences we're creating for audiences, and sharing around the world.

18

Teaching Physical Improv

Over many years' teaching players of all experience levels, I've found a few unique issues with environment and object work. If you're planning to add more physical improv instruction to your classes, the following notes may help you and your students.

Tools Not Rules

I've talked enough about improv rules (way back in Chapter 2). However, it's important we remain aware of how easily students can convert loose guidelines into rigid methods. Because environment work feels unusual, many people use it only in the ways in which they are taught, rather than as a starting point for physical exploration.

In my classes, I continually refer back to my First Principles. I also remind students that, like all improvisers, I'm a work-in-progress—constantly learning and refining my approach. I teach the tools that have worked for me, but there are others, including things no one has even thought of as yet.

My main role is to help improvisers build their instincts for advancing a scene. How they choose to do it is always wide open.

Safety First

When I began studying improv at The Second City Training Centre, the studios had sheets of plywood screwed to the walls. I asked a teacher why, and was told it was because beginners often kicked, fell into, or threw chairs at the drywall. *"Improv gets pretty crazy sometimes"* was a common remark, often accompanied by a shrug.

Protecting the facilities was a good idea, but it might have been better to teach responsible impulse control in the first place. I never attacked a wall, but I did cause myself a few injuries before I started paying attention to this.

Physical and Emotional Safety for performers begins in the classroom. It's a delicate balancing act. We must teach physical commitment *and* knowing your limits, spontaneity *and* impulse control, risking failure *and* being accountable for your actions. Students must understand that *"anything can happen in improv"* does not mean that every behavior is safe or acceptable.

Model both types of safety in your classes. When issues arise, point them out and discuss. Help students understand their responsibility to the work and to each other.

Developing Physicality

The first hurdle in teaching physical improv is getting students to *be more physical*. Most people have been conditioned by society to avoid acting out. And even with training, experienced improvisers sometimes become static in performance. Overcoming these learned behaviors isn't a quick process.

Movement drills are fundamental to students connecting with their bodies. Allow lots of time for physical warm-ups, and let them play out if students show involvement with the activity. I've sometimes played improvised dodge ball for ten minutes or more. Viola Spolin claimed to have seen children play as many as five innings of improvised baseball. Also use warm-ups between scene work exercises and anytime energy seems to be dropping.

Many Where exercises are played in silence to allow focus on movement. If overused, though, this teaches players that physicality is separate from dialogue. *Gibberish* is always an option—it forces improvisers to communicate physically while they speak. Students experience how movement can affect dialogue and vice versa, and work with both to be more expressive. Spolin's *Improvisation for the Theater* describes a series of Gibberish exercises, but you can really use it anytime. The important thing is to make sure it's spoken sound without content. Students should avoid using real foreign languages or creating their own from repeated Gibberish sounds.

Also be aware that students sometimes lose connection with group play as they build physicality, especially if you teach a lot of solo or parallel exercises. They may focus on their own environment work too much, and/or find it hard to give and take with others. Remind scene partners to play with each other (as I described in Chapter 2).

Say What You See

A player's ability to be physical goes beyond their knowledge of tools and awareness of opportunities to use them. Students are also affected by mobility challenges, negative body image, cultural expectations, or fear of embarrassment. Sometimes they aren't even aware of these influences.

Because of this, when students have trouble with object work, resist telling them how to do it, or side-coaching them to move in specific ways. There may be unseen reasons why they can't comply. Or, they may limit their growth by internalizing your instructions as a "rule." They may even risk injuring themselves physically or emotionally.

Instead, simply tell them what you see. External observations are valuable feedback for students learning to communicate physically. When side-coaching, try to guide them toward discovery. If an object or activity isn't clear, prompt them to think of other details to include. If they seem stuck in a scene, remind them to explore the space. Help each student find their own path into physicality.

Plan to Adapt

Be flexible in your lesson planning to serve students' needs. Stretching their skills is an important part of training, but if they're clearly struggling, switching to a different exercise can help. To do this well, you need to know a wide variety of games and their uses. Plan several backups and alternatives, and keep a long list of warm-ups ready for use anytime. To explore a specific problem that comes up, you may want to abandon your plan completely.

Sometimes I'll ask students to improvise by narrating thought experiments rather than acting out scenes. In their imagination they will sometimes take more risks, which mentally prepares them for more physicality on the stage. (Spolin's *Verbalizing the Where* exercise, on page 189, is very useful.)

Also be ready to adapt when safety issues arise. Discussion helps players learn the nuances of responsible performance. This may take away from your current lesson, but it's more valuable in the long term.

Play

Of all the benefits of physical improv I've written about in this book, I think the greatest is that it encourages play. As long as it's in a safe, respectful environment, play helps students develop and explore instincts without all the *thinking* that plagues improvisers.

One of my best object work exercises is *Improv Basketball*. (You'll find it in the Appendix on page 179.) To pass the ball, you have to be clear about where and how you're sending it. If you're sloppy, you get instant feedback when other players follow it in a different direction. Unclear object work sometimes splits the ball into two, as different players each think they've grabbed it. Most often, they figure out how to resolve possession on their own. If not, it's a great opportunity to teach preserving an established reality. In giving up "their" ball, players also learn about character agendas and letting go of ideas to serve the scene.

But more than all this, basketball creates goofy behavior. Players will dribble between their legs, or spin the ball on their finger. Someone might become a referee and start calling fouls. A student of mine once started whistling the Harlem Globetrotters theme. Everyone is completely in the moment, full of joy, and nothing feels like a forced gag.

Environment work brings this spirit of play into any improvisation. Our blank stage is the treehouse we transform into starships, jungles, and haunted houses. Prompt your students to play in their worlds. Have them mischievously rifle through someone else's stuff. Get them to break things. Create literal obstacles to their existential goals. Scenes may fail, but this teaches valuable lessons in storytelling. Once students get a taste of play from environment work, they'll find it elsewhere in their improv.

Finally, be playful in your *instruction*. I "invented" improv basketball on a day when my class was bored of tossing yet another space ball around the circle. Of course, I was embarrassed to discover Spolin was playing basketball with her students before I was even born. But in being open to play, I stumbled across a powerful exercise I might have otherwise missed.

Modern improv needs more play. Even for beginners, a workshop should be more laboratory than factory.

Final Thoughts

Like many improv scenes, a book is never really finished. Someone just takes the lights down, hopefully with good timing. Before I exit this stage, a few parting words.

Two Big Takeaways

The biggest thing I hope you take away from this book is a greater commitment to safety in improv performance. There aren't enough easy-to-find, comprehensive resources out there. Until there are, our community needs players like you to pay attention and spread the word on these issues.

My second takeaway for you is the importance of clear and specific object work, every time you use it. That said, *every time* doesn't mean you should use it *all the time*. Constantly playing with objects and activities soon becomes as limiting as no physicality at all. Remember that physical improv is only part of a well-rounded skill set.

I can't stress enough the importance of regularly practicing your skills. Safety and muscle memory are the best reasons, but so is mindset. When you regularly give thought to where you are, it opens up worlds of choice for your improvisation. Not every scene needs environment, but practice keeps you ready to explore it when you need to.

A New Process

If you like the ideas in this book, you may resolve to "be more physical" with your improv from now on. Fantastic! But don't be surprised if this seems difficult at first. Your instincts won't change overnight, or after reading a book, or even with weeks of classes. It's a long, slow process of reacting to moments in performance and learning from how they play out.

Embrace this process. Experiment and find your own balance. Fail spectacularly. People will still love you for trying something different. Even if you make just one scene in your next show a little more physical, that's still enough to delight a crowd.

Standing Out and Fitting In

Despite the advantages I've described, you'll find that large pockets of our community still don't give their physical improv skills much thought. If you want to work as a professional improviser, this is both good and bad.

It's good because developing your physical play helps you stand out. We love to think of improv as this democratic utopia where all players are equal. The reality is, no audience wants everyone to be the same. When you play in a different way, you add value to the show by mixing things up.

Let's also acknowledge that, as a professional, you *have* to find ways to stand out. Throughout your career, you'll compete for jobs and stage time with many other actors. You need a well-rounded skill set, but leaning into what you do differently gives you an edge.

The only sin is *shining*—deliberately playing to highlight your performance at the expense of other players and often the scene itself. Be generous with your improv, always. Stay connected with your partners, accept their offers, and don't bulldoze scenes with your physicality. A generous physical improviser is a powerful addition to any team.

I must warn you, however, that not all improvisers feel this way. Some think of environment work as silly and gimmicky, a tool for showing off. In my career I've seen loads of unprofessional behavior: actors mocking others behind their back, instructors coaching students to *"cut out that mime shit."* I hope you never experience situations like these.

As important as standing out may be in the professional sphere, it's equally important to understand group culture and expectations. If you're entering a new community, or preparing for an audition, do your research. Watch a few shows. Chat about style with players and producers. Keep your eyes and ears open.

As a newbie, in some cases it may be necessary to shift your approach to fit in with the group or community. You can dial back your physicality while still holding true to the philosophy of environment. As you become more established, you can shift back to more physical play. Maybe you'll make a few converts along the way!

Now It's Your Turn

Over my career, I've had extraordinary training and experiences in improvisation. Even so, I wouldn't be where I am today without the countless hours spent simply talking about it with my students and fellow players. We've told stories, debated theories, and suggested new ideas. I've learned so much from these conversations.

I'd love to start a conversation with *you*! Please visit my website, https:// improvillusionist.com, and let me know what you think of the material in this book. I've always thought of it as a starting point, an opening offer that others can build on. I can't wait to see where we take physical improv together.

Thank you for your ideas, your talent, and your commitment to this art form we all love. Now get out there and show us the next great improv illusion!

Want to Learn More about Physical Improv?

Check out the *Improv Illusionist* website and get **special bonuses** exclusively for book owners!

- *The Director's Cut*: More notes about important topics in the book.
- Video examples for object work practice and environment work exercises.
- Information on Physical Improv workshops (in-person and online).
- Monthly *Improv Illusionist* Newsletter.
- Priority access to new content.
- Email access to the author—ask me anything!

Get all this now at: https://improvillusionist.com/book-bonus

Appendix
Exercises

These are some of my favorite exercises and performance games for physical improv. Many of them are old classics, and some are experimental ones I've made up. You might know them by different names—similar games often have local variations.

I'm listing these in the order I might teach them over the course of a multi-day workshop. The later ones aren't necessarily more advanced, but they may have concepts that layer onto earlier ones.

Improv exercises are widely shared and it's hard to attribute them to their creators. If I've made a mistake, or you can help name the innovator for future editions of this book, please contact me via the *Improv Illusionist* website.

If you come across any exercises that work well for training these skills, please send them to me! I'd love to make use of them and include them in future editions of this book.

Warm-ups

Space Substance/Space Shaping (Viola Spolin)

Working solo, players stand with palms facing each other, moving hands closer together and further apart, focusing on the space between. This is not rigid, aimless hand-waving. Really try to feel the "space stuff" between your hands.

Next, try working with a partner to sense the space substance between you. You can also explore moving through space, feeling it with your whole body.

Once you have some experience with space substance, try shaping it with your hands, arms, and body. Allow it to take shape as an object, if it does, but don't force it.

(Read more about Attitude on page 28.)

Play Ball (Viola Spolin)

Players stand in a circle and agree on a size/type of improvised ball, then toss it among themselves. Focus on consistency—keep the ball the same size, shape, and weight at all times. The coach can call out instructions to change the properties of the ball.

What do you notice about how people move with the ball, and how does this relate to "seeing" it?

(Read more about Object Interactions on page 31.)

Hot Potato

Instead of a ball, players toss an improvised hot potato. Play the reality of size, shape, and heat. It's not something you can hold onto for long, and catching it will cause a reaction. You can also try this with other objects of odd shape or discomfort: a bowling pin, a spiky sea urchin, a heavy medicine ball, etc.

Red Ball

Great for new improvisers, similar to *Play Ball*. Players toss an improvised ball around the circle, calling out the ball's color: *"Red Ball."* Call it out when you throw *and* when you catch—this is key to understanding each player's responsibility for clearly communicating an idea. To increase challenge, the coach can add more balls of different colors. This makes it even more important to call back the color of the ball when receiving it.

Energy Ball

Similar to *Play Ball,* toss a ball of energy around the circle. Players "charge" the ball up or down before throwing. Focus on catching the ball with the same energy as that of the thrower. For fun, players can add crackling energy sound effects.

Loser Ball (Jill Bernard)

Similar to *Play Ball*, except there are two rules. First, no one can catch the ball. Second, everyone enthusiastically supports everyone else's inability to catch the ball. (e.g., *"You can do it! Yay! Great job! You'll get it next time!"*) Beyond teaching players to fail enthusiastically, this is actually a great way to practice object work, since it takes an equal amount of effort to show us you're *missing* the ball as it does to show you're catching it. Try alternating this with the more realistic *Play Ball*.

Transformation of Objects (Viola Spolin)

Players stand in a circle. Player 1 creates an object and passes it on. Player 2 transforms the object into something else, and so on. Players should receive and play with an object first, to discover a change instead of thinking one up and forcing it. Associations don't count either—creating a mirror to use with a comb isn't a transformation. Work with the motion of the previous object to help the transformation.

(Read more about Training Your Instinct on page 34.)

Object Toss

One of my favorite catch games. Players name any small object they can think of, and then toss it across the circle, for example, a hammer, a fried egg sandwich, a loose deck of cards, a goldfish in a bag. Try to keep the object consistent as you throw and catch. Once the receiving player catches the object, they call out a new one.

(Read more about Training Your Instinct on page 34.)

Pass 4

Four objects are passed (not necessarily thrown) around a circle at the same time: a baseball, an inflatable beach ball, a heavy medicine ball, and a sleeping baby. Play the reality of each object. Everyone should work extra hard to protect the baby!

Yes, Let's!

Players stand in a circle. One player calls out any activity; for example, *"Let's . . . play tennis!"* All others call back, *"Yes, let's!"* Then everyone performs the activity for a few moments. Then another player calls out a different activity, and so on.

Encourage players to think creatively about how they show the activity, avoiding clichés. For example, when someone calls out *"Let's play baseball!"* nearly everyone either pitches or bats. You could also show us an outfielder waiting, or the umpire, or even someone in the stands watching.

Dodge Ball (Viola Spolin)

Players in a circle pass around an improvised ball, trying to hit one player in the center. If the center player is "hit," change places with the person who threw it. A hit above the waist is a foul. Allow players to work out judgment calls for themselves. Focus on consistency of the ball, which is more important than "winning."

Three-Person Tableau

Players stand in a circle. Player 1 enters the circle and poses as a statue, declaring what they are; for example, *"I'm a tree."* Player 2 adds to the picture as a complementary feature of the first object; for example, *"I'm a bird in the tree."* Player 3 adds another complementary feature; for example, *"I'm a cowering worm."* Once you have three, Player 1 chooses one of the other two statues to remain while the others clear. Start again with that statue.

(Read more about the Power of Three on page 104.)

Three Elements Pinball

Players stand in a circle, using an improvised basketball. Player 1 passes to anyone, calling out a type of suggestion you might ask from an audience, for example, *"Location!"* Player 2 passes to anyone, providing the suggestion, for example, *"An office!"* Player 3 holds the ball while they call out three elements of that suggestion, for example, *"Desk! Computer! Loud co-worker!"* Any elements related to the suggestion are fine—they don't have to be original. We're looking for speed. When finished, Player 3 passes to anyone, and the cycle starts over.

Encourage spontaneity to keep the ball moving fast. Also, keep an eye on the consistency of the ball. As players stop to think, they may lose focus and unconsciously change the object.

Once players get good at this, the coach can optionally stop them occasionally, getting the player to pick one of their three elements and start a scene.

Note that players 1 and 2 often find it just as challenging to select the category and example. This is a good illustration of why we need to think in advance about the suggestions we'll want to ask for in a show.

(Read more about the Three Elements Technique on page 106.)

Butterfly Nets

A nice one for young children, but useful for anyone to practice slowing down and lightness of movement. Imagine the space is a lush garden, filled with butterflies. Players use nets to catch butterflies, take them in hand and examine them, then release. Focus on a delicate touch.

Improv Basketball

Treat the space as a basketball court, with nets at opposite ends. Players choose sides and play. Watch for consistency of ball handling, and be careful not to split the ball into more than one. Players who can't or don't want to join the game can fill in the stage picture: referees, fans, etc.

Coaches: Set this up quickly, with as little explanation as possible. Maybe just point out where the two nets are, then let the players figure out for themselves how to play.

Follow the Leader/Boot Camp/Tough Mudder

Imagine the space as a playground or army base or obstacle race. Players follow a leader up, down, over, and under various obstacles. Play with how you pass by these obstacles, but try to keep things consistent—the same size, shape, and in the same place. The leader should be mindful of mobility and flexibility issues in the class. This one is VERY physical.

(Read more about Finding More Play on page 13.)

What Are You Doing?

Players work in pairs. Player 1 asks the other: *"What are you doing?"* Player 2 replies with any activity; for example, *"I'm digging a hole."* Player 1 plays that activity. Then Player 2 asks, *"What are you doing?"* Player 1 replies with a different activity to the one they're currently doing. Continue back and forth. You can also adapt this for a large group in a circle.

Solo Exercises

Muscle Memory

Grab any small (real) object that's within reach. How does your arm move to pick it up? How do the fingers curl around it? Is it heavy or light? Do you have to grip it hard to lift, or do you have a light touch? Let go and notice the release. Pick it up and put it down a few times to notice how it feels. Try it with different speed and energy. Think about what changes and what stays the same.

Notice also that some objects have connected movements. When you drink from a cup, not only does your arm move, your lips do too, and so does your throat as you swallow. These connections are often the A-level specifics that create an illusion.

Now try those same motions again *without the object.* See how easy it is to reproduce the detail?

You can practice this anytime you pick up a real-world object. Just put it down and repeat the same movements with a space object. Be careful not to strain your muscles, or become too reliant on a specific pattern of movement.

(Read more about Muscle Memory on page 33.)

Begin and End with Objects (Viola Spolin)

(Described in detail on page 38.) A very important exercise for improving object work. Learn to break down the individual movements and make them clear and specific.

Powering through Obstacles

A single player picks any improvised activity, for example, paddling a canoe, and commits to performing it as realistically as possible. The coach calls out various problems as obstacles to the activity: for example, *"The paddle breaks!"* or *"The canoe is sinking!"* or *"You're attacked by mosquitoes!"* No matter what happens, the player must adapt to keep performing the activity. Avoid "magical" solutions to problems—stay in the moment and play the reality as much as possible. As a fully solo exercise, the player themself can introduce their own obstacles.

(Read more about The Solution to bad habits on page 55.)

Clothing Trouble

Choose various types of improvised clothes. Practice putting them on or taking them off. Look for small "trouble" details like pulling on fabric or working with zippers and buttons.

(Read more about Trouble on page 39.)

What's Next?

Single player or a group of players working separately. Choose a simple activity that takes more than a few steps to accomplish, for example, making a sandwich, loading a laundry machine. The coach or observers call out a first step, which the player performs any way they interpret. Then the coach calls *"What's Next?"* to get a next step, and so on. Note how people approach activities in different ways—one person's next step may not be the same as another's. Have the players use the suggestions from the audience instead of their own ideas—it helps them see things differently.

(Read more about Thinking in Routines on page 44.)

Breaking Routines

The player chooses and performs an activity routine, which they then perform without incident. Repeat the routine, but this time find two ways to break it (i.e., things go wrong). The first break is minor—they can fix or ignore it and continue. The second break is catastrophic and ends the activity.

For fun, you can do this as a Die game—the second break kills the character somehow. Encourage players to avoid the obvious choice, like stabbing themselves while cutting vegetables. (I don't recommend you use this variation when working with children. They will often make an extreme choice at the expense of the exercise and risk hurting themselves.)

(Read more about Breaking Routines on page 47.)

Difficulty with Small Objects (Viola Spolin)

A single player becomes involved with a small object or a piece of clothing, for example, opening a pill bottle, fixing a stuck zipper. This can be expanded to involve two or more players working together.

(Read more about Trouble on page 39.)

Focused Work

A variation on *Difficulty with Small Objects*. A single player chooses and performs an activity with small objects and very fine detail, for example, needlepoint, painting tiny figurines, building a model airplane. Maintain this activity while carrying on a conversation, with the coach or another player working separately.

Coaches: Watch for repetition or loss of detail, which are hints that the player is losing focus.

(Read more about Trouble on page 39 and Remembering Your Eye Contact on page 64.)

At the Gym

A good exercise for muscle memory practice. Show us how you might lift weights at the gym, without physically tensing your muscles. Try different weights, types, and sizes. Are you using free weights or machines? Be careful not to "lift" too much—protect yourself from injury!

(Read more about Danger #1: Muscle Strains on page 35.)

Trapped (Viola Spolin)

A single player chooses a small, contained environment from which to escape, for example, a bear trap, a stuck elevator. For added challenge, you could add a character element. How might a mouse escape from a mousetrap?

Coaches: Be careful with this one—players will often strain themselves trying to pull free, which can cause injury. Learn to show effort without physically tensing the muscles.

(Read more about Trouble on page 39 and Danger #1: Muscle Strains on page 35.)

Noting Your Physicality

Single player starts with a space object. They handle the object and let it help them make strong decisions about character and location. Expand the activities to further define Who they are and Where.

Do this exercise slowly at first. The coach can prompt if the player seems stuck. Some example prompts: *"Are you doing it fast or slow?" "Is it important to you?" "Do you like this activity?"* Continue to prompt, *"What does that suggest?"*

(Read more about Noting and Making Choices on page 62.)

Exploring Activity Movements

A solo player chooses an activity. As they perform it, choose any single movement that reoccurs as part of the activity. Keeping the overall activity, the player then explores changing up that movement, for example, making it faster/slower, harder/gentler, bigger/smaller. The coach can provide direction if necessary.

Notice how changes to the movement can suggest changes to character.

(Read more about Focusing on How instead of Why on page 65.)

Exploring Activity Attitudes

A solo player chooses an activity. The player continues to perform the activity as the coach calls out various attitudes they must take on. (Try some of these: satisfied, proud, excited, enthusiastic, confident, uncomfortable, bored, resentful, guilty, suspicious, secretive, anxious, disgusted, or any others you can think of.) Try to balance positive and negative attitudes.

Notice how changes to the attitude can completely change the activity. You can explore that point-of-view for even more ideas within scenes.

(Read more about Changing Your Attitude on page 65.)

Physicalizing an Object (Viola Spolin)

A single player chooses an object, animate or inanimate, and handles it. They must communicate the life and movement of the object. This requires use of the whole body, not only the hands. Examples include a yo-yo, pinball machine, or hamster.

What's Beyond? (Viola Spolin)

A single player moves across the stage making an entrance and exit. They must show what location they have left and where they are going to. Think of the stage as a bare hallway you're using for the transition. No extra action takes place here other than to show what's beyond the entrance and exit.

(Read more about What's Beyond? on page 78.)

Group Exercises

Consent Practice Exercises (Kaci Beeler)

(See page 140 and the rest of the chapter on Emotional Safety.) Introduce Consent Practice and Boundaries Conversations early and often. Use them in workshops, rehearsals, and shows. Help create safer spaces for all improvisers.

Poison-Arm Samurai

The group enacts a sword battle in slow-motion. Each player's outstretched arm is their "sword"—dipped in poison, one touch is lethal. Play everything in slow-motion—attacks, deaths, taunting opponents.

Watch for players speeding up to strike or avoid a touch. Discuss pursuing a personal agenda (surviving the game) at the cost of the reality of the scene (the slow-motion). Challenge players to risk getting caught, or allowing someone to get away, while remaining slow. Emphasize the importance of safety with stage violence.

(Read more about Violence on page 126.)

Trading Punches

Have players pair up and practice trading slow-motion punches, back and forth (*using the techniques described on page 126*). Encourage them to move even more slowly than they think they should. *Players should never physically connect, even slowly.* Let the receiving player practice "taking" the punch, being careful not to strain.

After this has been well practiced, the receiving players can optionally try falling down—again in slow-motion (*as described in the section on Falls on page 129*).

Back-to-Back Activity

Two players. Give one player a real object and associated activity. It shouldn't be too complex but should involve a few steps. Common examples include taking off one lace-up shoe and putting it back on again, or retrieving an object from a backpack. Let the other player study the object for a moment. They will perform exactly the same activity using object work.

Stand the players facing away, so they can't see each other; then both start at the same time. Do the activity at regular speed—this isn't a race. Ideally, you should see the same level of detail from both players, and they should finish at the same time. More likely, the object work player will finish first, with far less detail. Discuss the differences you observe.

(*Read more about Hand-waving on page 52.*)

Sub-locations

This is a casual exercise for thinking about specificity. Choose a generic location and brainstorm as many different sub-locations as the group can come up with. You can choose to expand any of these out into scenes.

Long-form groups can also use this exercise as the basis for improvised plays. Establish characters at different sub-locations, and then have them run into each other as they travel through the "world."

The Where Game (Viola Spolin)

An excellent beginner's exercise. Player 1 decides on a location and shows Where through an object or activity. When an outside player thinks they know Where, they can assume a character and enter the location. Players establish relationships with the location and each other through objects. Keep the focus on the environment—character is secondary in this exercise.

(Read more about Placement on page 70.)

Fix a Problem, Leave a Problem

Decide on a location in advance. Each player passes through, one by one, contacting all objects established. Each player discovers one problem in the environment that they fix, for example, water puddle on the floor, broken doorknob. They also create one different problem and leave it behind. Players don't have to establish new objects but will probably have to. There can be more than one problem at a time, but keeping track of too many problems will make things difficult. Watch for consistency of objects: doors opening the same way, etc.

(Read more about Placement on page 70.)

Setting the Scene (Katy Schutte/Tim Sniffen)

Player 1 chooses a physical task and begins performing it. Player 2 commentates on everything they see Player 1 doing. They don't add anything to the scene or try to guess the task. If Player 2 is unsure of what they are seeing, they should say that. Provides instant object work feedback to Player 1, and trains Player 2 to focus on their partner.

Vocal Sound Effects (Viola Spolin)

Four to six players agree on a Where, then use sound only to communicate it. (They could be sitting down, or concealed behind a curtain, or the audience could close their eyes.)

(Read more about Sound Effects on page 83.)

Showing Who through the Use of Objects (Viola Spolin)

Three players decide on a group of characters or a simple relationship, for example, scientists, cleaners, guard/prisoners, or tourists/guide. Then, through the use of one or more objects, show the audience who those characters are. Afterward, discuss the specific objects or actions that clearly communicated information.

I sometimes combine this exercise with *Noting Your Physicality* (in the *Solo Exercises* section above) to help players develop characters from the environment. Here they show not only the character types but also individual personalities.

(Read more about Character and Personality on page 96.)

Conversation with Involvement (Viola Spolin)

Two or three players. They agree on a simple topic of discussion and keep it going while they eat and drink a large meal. Keep the focus on eating and talking so this doesn't become a "scene" that avoids the exercise. Show the objects on the table. Chew and swallow your food!

Try this also with a larger group as a dinner party. Players can decide who they are as a group and individually. Everyone should stay engaged in a conversation, even if there is more than one around the table.

(Read more about Remembering Your Eye Contact on page 64.)

Conducted Story with Action/Color/ Emotion

A game for three players, or divide a larger number into groups of three who take turns within their group. A conductor points to players in turn, each continuing to tell a story from where the previous player left off. Each player (or group) has a fixed responsibility for elements of the story.

Player 1: Action—something happening in the story.

Player 2: Color—description of locations, characters, or events.

Player 3: Emotion—description of how characters feel about things.

Observe the importance of all these to tell a well-rounded story.

Murder Chain

A game for four players. All but one leave the room. Player 1 gets a location, an occupation, and an object. Player 2 enters from outside, and Player 1 has one minute to communicate the three items through actions and speech in Gibberish. The coach should update players on the time and encourage them to keep moving to cover all three items. Encourage Player 2 to make strong assumptions. At the end of one minute, Player 2 ends the scene by killing Player 1 with the object they think they have. Player 3 enters and it's Player 2's turn to communicate the three items they think they have. Repeat with Players 3 and 4. At the end, review in reverse order what each player thinks the items were, then reveal the originals.

This isn't a great game for performance, but useful for practicing clear, specific object work. It's interesting to see how ideas change when passed around. Discuss ways in which the information could have been more accurately communicated.

Where without Hands (Viola Spolin)

Two or more players decide on an object, which they have to handle or set in motion without using their hands. Objects or activities that don't usually need hands (e.g., stomping grapes) aren't allowed.

Showing Where without Objects (Viola Spolin)

Think about other ways to show environment without relying on physical objects. Two players show an environment using any of the following: seeing, listening, relationship, sound effects, lighting effects, or activity.

Spolin recommends delaying this exercise until students understand how to show Where through Who and What.

Animal Characters

Practice as a group. Everyone chooses an animal, and moves about the space as that animal. The animals don't interact. Take time to play with the physical movements of the animal.

This exercise can also help you create new characters. Gradually, each player becomes more human while keeping aspects of the original animal. Explore how you can develop characters with animal-like traits. A mousy person might be timid, and alternate between freezing still and darting around the room. A lion might lazily sit around, but become ferocious when bothered. What does it really mean for someone to be "bull-headed?"

(Read more about Playing Animals and Objects on page 88.)

Exploration of a Larger Environment/ Weather Exercise (Viola Spolin)

Players choose an outdoor location and agree on characters and activity. They then explore the environment. Players should be affected by conditions beyond the immediate space. What is above? What is Below? Be affected by weather and outdoor conditions. Try to show as much as you can without using dialogue.

(Read more about The Great Outdoors on page 86.)

Scene Work

Note: *For many scene exercises, vocal expression or dialogue is optional. This helps beginning students focus more on the environment. Gibberish is always an option for training improvisers to be more physically expressive while they speak. (See the section on Developing Physicality on page 167 for more notes on Gibberish.)*

Verbalizing the Where (Viola Spolin)

Two or more players agree on the basic Where, Who, and What for a scene, then sit in chairs. Without moving from their seats, they verbalize the scene, narrating their actions. When speaking dialogue, they interrupt their narration to speak directly to others. Players verbalize everything in present tense, and narrate only their own actions, not others'. Stay in the Where and avoid narrating attitudes or judgments.

Once players can do this well, they then get up and play the same scene with physical actions, no longer narrating but still speaking dialogue as necessary.

Location Tour (Viola Spolin)

Spolin has many exercises involving detailed stage floor plans. This is a lighter version for creating improvised sets. As "homework," players study a room in their home, office, or other familiar place. They commit to memory as much detail about the furniture and objects as they can. In class, they give a tour of the room as it would fit on the stage, placing objects and describing the layout. After the tour, other players can join to perform a scene in that location.

(Read more about Pre-Fab Sets on page 72.)

Location Tour (Katy Schutte Variation)

During the tour, player adds stories (real or fictional) about why some items are there. This provides additional background, which may be useful in the following scene.

(Read more about Pre-Fab Sets on page 72.)

Location Tour with Movie Scenes

Similar to *Location Tour*, except that here students study a clip from their favorite film or TV show. Commit to memory as much detail about the scene as possible. In class, describe the environment as an improvised set. After describing, add other students to perform a scene in that location. If special effects or camera tricks are used, can you replicate them?

(Read more about Movie Magic on page 84.)

Where with Set Pieces (Viola Spolin)

Create a list of props and furniture. Teams of players create different scenes using the same list of objects. Experiment with agreeing where the props are in advance, or starting with just the list in mind. Try to let the Where create the scene, rather than impose a scene on the objects.

(Read more about Pre-Fab Sets on page 72.)

Finding Objects in the Immediate Environment (Viola Spolin)

Three or more players agree on a simple group relationship and a topic of discussion. While the discussion proceeds, each player must handle objects found in the environment. Try not to invent objects, but rather discover them. Keep the discussion going! There should be dozens of objects by the end.

(Read more about Looking Around on page 82.)

Create an Object, Say a Line

Two or three players. Like *Finding Objects in the Immediate Environment* above, but players can choose any location, characters, and activity. They can speak a next line of dialogue only after they have established a new object in the environment. It must be a new object, not a new activity or new use for the same object.

(Read more about Looking Around on page 82.)

Aligned/Misaligned Relationship

Two players choose a relationship and an activity they can do together. Throughout the scene they handle objects related to the activity. Observe each other and handle objects the same way (aligned). At some point, the coach calls out "*Shift!*" and the players now handle objects in different ways of their choosing (misaligned).

Talk about how the relationship and dynamic appear to change, even if the characters change nothing else about their behavior.

(Read more about Relationship and Dynamic on page 97.)

Follow-on Scenes

One group of two to four players does a scene establishing a location with several objects. Then a second group plays a scene in the same location, at some time after the first. Location starts as it was at the end of the previous scene. The second scene will likely have some relation to the first, but it doesn't have to. Watch for consistency of the objects and activities.

The Specialized Where (Viola Spolin)

Players get a generic location, for example, office, classroom, kitchen. Then they decide on a more specific setting to show the audience, for example, swamp office, outer-space classroom, a kitchen in Hell. They can agree in advance on Who they are and What they're doing.

Of course you can experiment, but this is usually best played by carrying out the common activities of the generic location, layering on the added perspective of the unusual setting.

(Read more about the Three Elements Technique on page 106.)

Stage Picture (Background)

Two or three players in a location where other people are commonly present. As they play a scene, other players should step in to occupy the background, filling in the stage picture. They can be stationary or passing through. Background players should be "alive" but not distracting.

(Read more about Stage Picture on page 67.)

Radio (Viola Spolin)

In one variation of this exercise, three or more players decide on a Where, then play a scene by voice and sound alone. (They could be sitting down, or concealed behind a curtain, or the audience could close their eyes.) Players should add vocal sound effects to enhance the action. If a technical improviser is available, they can assist with adding sound.

(Read more about Technical Assistance on page 74 and Sound Effects on page 83.)

Human Props

Two or three players start a scene with any information they want. Throughout, they discover objects or creatures in the scene. Other players join to become those objects, which the characters handle (safely). Outside players can also jump in as objects and allow the characters in the scene to discover what they are.

(Read more about Playing Animals and Objects on page 88.)

Scene-Painting Intros

Practice setting up scenes by describing a few things about the location to the audience. Then play the scene, making use of the described objects.

(Read more about Scene-Painting on page 79.)

Scene-Painting Curveballs

Have players start a scene. At one or more random points, have someone outside the scene describe something in the environment; for example, *"There's a beautiful portrait of her mother on the wall,"* or *"A large window looks out over the city skyline."* Be careful about abrupt changes, which draw focus and alter the scene; for example, *"A rock crashes through the window."* Let the people in the scene work with the new information, rather than push a new direction on them.

(Read more about Scene-Painting on page 79.)

Real Estate Tour

This exercise is excellent for experimenting with split-screens, levels, and changing locations. Play a scene where one player, a real estate agent, leads other players on a home tour. Move through different rooms, go up and down stairs, and play with objects in each room. Maybe a player lingers in one room while the rest of the group moves on. How well can you establish and remember the layout of the house?

(Read more about Physical Stage Effects in Chapter 13, beginning on page 111.)

Glossary of Improv Terms

Backline The group of improvisers not in the current scene, often standing in a line across the back of the stage, on either side, or even off-stage.

Blocking Denying an offer, such as when one player establishes a desk and then another walks right through that space. While it's often unintentional, sometimes improvisers deliberately block in an effort to maintain control. (Note that in formal theatre, blocking refers to stage movement worked out during the rehearsal process. In *Improvisation for the Theater*, Viola Spolin writes about "nondirectional blocking"—making purposeful stage movement look natural.)

Bridging Delaying the action of a scene when it's clear that the story is headed that way. It's possible this can be used for some types of stories (such as a quest), or to build suspense, but more often it causes boredom.

Business Any physical activity that creates atmosphere or characterization. Often used to give characters an impression of life when they're in the background of a scene, since standing there frozen looks unnatural.

Canceling Erasing an established offer, such as digging up a treasure chest but finding nothing inside. Improvisers often back off on offers, because they don't trust their ideas or are afraid of what happens next.

Editing Occurs when a player or director declares an end to a scene, through physical gesture (such as "sweeping" across the stage) or calling *"Scene!"* Occurs most often in formats where one scene gives way to another without a setup or audience interaction.

Endowment An offer from one player that lays information onto another. For example, if Player 2 enters the scene and Player 1 says, *"Good morning, Doctor,"* Player 2 has been *endowed* as a doctor, and should behave as that character; otherwise, they are *blocking*. Endowment can be misused to control a scene or manipulate partners.

Environment The "Where" of an improv scene, which includes the general location and the larger world. *Environment work* is the set of skills for giving an improvisation a sense of place.

Long-form A category of improv performance where the whole show is meant to be one unified experience. Individual scenes may tell a larger story, or ideas from one scene inform the others. In long-form, there is usually little audience interaction.

Object Work   Also known as *mime*, the skill of using your hands, body, and movement to create "implied objects," which take the place of real props in improvisation.

Offer   Any idea that advances an improv scene. Offers can be made physically, through dialogue, or any other way that communicates information. Improvisers can even make offers unconsciously, if an idea is noticed and received by their scene partner.

Physical Improv   Any improv technique that creates an illusion of physical objects, activities, and locations that aren't really there. This is not limited to movement and physicality. Depending on the situation, even dialogue or emotional reactions can do it. For example, shuddering in terror as you describe a tornado bearing down on you is a perfectly legitimate example of physical improv.

Platform   The initial information that orients a scene, which may include Who, What, and Where, though none of those are necessarily required.

Routine   The physical steps taken in carrying out any given activity. In *Impro for Storytellers*, Keith Johnstone uses a broader definition: it's *anything* the characters are doing.

Short-form   A category of improv performance where scenes are a few minutes long and usually unrelated to each other. In short-form, performers usually interact with the audience to introduce each scene and get suggestions.

Sidetracking   Diverting from the goal of a story, often from fear of taking a step in that direction.

Space Object   Any improvised, "implied" object handled by a character, created using *object work*.

Steamrolling   Attempting to take over a scene by pushing your ideas and/or agenda to the exclusion of other players. Usually a reaction to fear that the scene is dying, or that not enough is happening.

Trouble   Something about an object or activity that keeps you from working with it 100 percent smoothly. Fixing the trouble could be simple (e.g., cleaning a smudge from your glasses) or it could break the routine (e.g., digging a hole and the shovel breaks).

Bibliography

Besser, Matt, Ian Roberts, and Matt Walsh. *The Upright Citizens Brigade Comedy Improvisation Manual*. 1st ed. New York: Comedy Council of Nicea, 2013.

Halpern, Charna, Del Close, and Kim Johnson. *Truth in Comedy: The Manual of Improvisation*. 1st ed. Colorado Springs, CO: Meriwether Publishing, 1994.

Johnstone, Keith. *Impro: Improvisation and the Theatre*. London: Eyre Methuen, 1981.

Johnstone, Keith. *Impro for Storytellers*. New York: Routledge/Theatre Arts Books, 1999.

Libera, Anne, ed. *The Second City Almanac of Improvisation*. Evanston, IL: Northwestern University Press, 2004.

Martinez, J. D. *Combat Mime: A Non-Violent Approach to Stage Violence*. Chicago, IL: Nelson-Hall, 1982.

Napier, Mick. *Improvise: Scene from the Inside Out*. 2nd ed. Denver, CO: Meriwether Publishing, A division of Pioneer Drama Service, Inc., 2015.

Paul, Annie Murphy. *The Extended Mind: The Power of Thinking Outside the Brain*. Boston, MA: Houghton Mifflin Harcourt, 2021.

Salinsky, Tom, and Deborah Frances-White. *The Improv Handbook: The Ultimate Guide to Improvising in Comedy, Theater, and Beyond*. New York: Continuum, 2008.

Schutte, Katy. *The Improviser's Way: A Longform Workbook*. London: Nick Hearn Books, 2018.

Scruggs, Mary, and Michael J. Gellman. *Process: An Improviser's Journey*. Evanston, IL: Northwestern University Press, 2008.

Spolin, Viola. *Theater Games for the Classroom: A Teacher's Handbook*. Evanston, IL: Northwestern University Press, 1986.

Spolin, Viola. *Improvisation for the Theater: A Handbook of Teaching and Directing Techniques*. 3rd ed. Evanston, IL: Northwestern University Press, 1999.

Stiles, Patti. *Improvise Freely: Throw Away the Rulebook and Unleash Your Creativity*. Melbourne: Big Toast Entertainment, 2021.

Index